2nd Workshop on Tools and Resources for REAding DIfficulties (READI 2022)

Held at LREC 2022

Marseille, France
20 – 25 June 2022

Editors:

Rodrigo Wilkens
David Alfter
Remi Cardon
Nuria Gala

ISBN: 978-1-7138-6144-7

Printed from e-media with permission by:

Curran Associates, Inc.
57 Morehouse Lane
Red Hook, NY 12571

Some format issues inherent in the e-media version may also appear in this print version.

Association for Computational Linguistics
209 N. Eighth Street
Stroudsburg, Pennsylvania 18360

Phone: 1-570-476-8006
Fax: 1-570-476-0860

acl@aclweb.org

Additional copies of this publication are available from:

Curran Associates, Inc.
57 Morehouse Lane
Red Hook, NY 12571 USA
Phone: 845-758-0400
Fax: 845-758-2633
Email: curran@proceedings.com
Web: www.proceedings.com

LREC 2022 Workshop
Language Resources and Evaluation Conference
20-25 June 2022

2nd Workshop on Tools and Resources for READing DIfficulties (READI)

Editors:
Rodrigo Wilkens, David Alfter, Rémi Cardon and Núria Gala

Proceedings of the LREC 2022 workshop on Tools and Resources with REAding DIfficulties (READI)

Edited by:
Rodrigo Wilkens, David Alfter, Rémi Cardon and Núria Gala

For more information:
European Language Resources Association (ELRA)
9 rue des Cordelires
75013, Paris
France
http://www.elra.info
Email: lrec@elda.org

Message from the General Chair

Recent studies show that the number of children and adults facing difficulties in reading and understanding written texts is steadily growing. Reading challenges can show up early on and may include reading accuracy, speed, or comprehension to the extent that the impairment interferes with academic achievement or activities of daily life. Various technologies (text customization, text simplification, text to speech devices, screening for readers through games and web applications, to name a few) have been developed to help poor readers to get better access to information as well as to support reading development. Among those technologies, text adaptations are a powerful way to leverage document accessibility by using NLP techniques.

The "Second Workshop on Tools and Resources for REAding DIfficulties" (READI), collocated with the "International Conference on Language Resources and Evaluation" (LREC 2022), aims at presenting current state-of-the-art techniques and achievements for text adaptations together with existing reading aids and resources for lifelong learning. The materials can be addressed to children struggling with difficulties in learning to read, to the community of teachers, speech-language pathologists and parents seeking solutions, but also to adults and professionals involved with adults struggling with reading (illiterates, aphasic readers, low vision readers, etc.).

In the second edition of READI, 14 propositions have been submitted from which 10 were accepted. Thus, the total rate of accepted papers is 71rate of 669, France 9, Switzerland 6, Iceland 5, Poland 4, Australia 3, Ireland 3, Spain 3, Sweden 3, Germany 2, Iran 1, Netherlands 1, United Kingdom 1, and Independent scholar 1). READI also features two invited speakers, Carolina Scarton (University of Sheffield, UK) and Arne Jönsson (Linköping University, Sweden). Moreover, we have decided to include in the program a one-hour slot for three papers from the 1st READI Workshop in 2020 (as the workshop could not take place due to the covid crisis).

We are thankful to the authors who submitted their work to this workshop, to our Program Committee members for their contributions, to the reviewers and the additional reviewers who did a thorough job evaluating submissions, to Carolina Scarton and Arne Jönsson who kindly accepted to be our invited speakers, and to LREC committee for including this workshop in their program. The workshop has been supported by Aix Marseille University, Laboratoire Parole et Langage (CNRS UMR 7309) and the Institute Language, Communication and the Brain (ILCB), funded by the French National Agency for Research (ANR, ANR-16-CONV-0002) and the Excellence Initiative of Aix- Marseille University A*MIDEX (ANR-11-IDEX-0001-02).

Organizers

David Alfter, Université catholique de Louvain, Belgium
Aurélie Calabrèse, Aix Marseille Université, France
Rémi Cardon, Université catholique de Louvain, Belgium
Thomas François, Université catholique de Louvain, Belgium
Núria Gala, Aix Marseille Université, France
Daria Goriachun, Aix Marseille Université, France
Horacio Saggion, Universitat Pompeu Fabra, Catalonia, Spain
Amalia Todirascu, Université de Strasbourg, France
Rodrigo Wilkens, Université catholique de Louvain, Belgium

Program Committee:

David Alfter, Université catholique de Louvain, Belgium
Delphine Bernhard, Université de Strasbourg, France
Aurélie Calabrèse, Aix Marseille Université, France
Rémi Cardon, Université catholique de Louvain, Belgium
Eric Castet, Aix Marseille Université, France
Thomas François, Université catholique de Louvain, Belgium
Núria Gala, Aix Marseille Université, France
Ludivine Javourey-Drevet, Université de Lille, France
Detmar Meurers, Universität Tübingen, Germany
Horacio Saggion, Universitat Pompeu Fabra, Catalonia, Spain
Matthew Shardlow, Manchester Metropolitan University, United Kingdom
Raffaele Spiezia, Università degli Studi della Campania "Luigi Vanvitelli", Italy
Anaïs Tack, Stanford University, US
Amalia Todirascu, Université de Strasbourg, France
Vincent Vandeghinste, Instituut voor de Nederlandse Taal, the Netherlands / University of Leuven, Belgium
Giulia Venturi, Istituto di Linguistica Computazionale A. Zampolli (ILC-CNR), Pisa, Italy
Aline Villavicencio, University of Sheffield, United Kingdom
Rodrigo Wilkens, Université catholique de Louvain, Belgium
Johannes C. Ziegler, Aix Marseille Université, France
Leonardo Zilio, University of Surrey, United Kingdom
Michael Zock, Aix Marseille Université, France

Invited Speakers:

Carolina Scarton, University of Sheffield, UK
Arne Jönsson, Linköping University, Sweden

Table of Contents

Conference Program

Friday, June 24, 2022

9:00–9:10 **Welcome**

9:10–10:00 **Invited speaker**

9:10–10:00 *Personalised Text Simplification*
Caroline Scarton

10:00–10:30 **Oral presentation**

10:00–10:30 *Reading Assistance through LARA, the Learning And Reading Assistant*
Elham Akhlaghi, Ingibjörg Iða Auðunardóttir, Branislav Bédi, Hakeem Beedar, Harald Berthelsen, Cathy Chua, Catia Cucchiarini, Brynjarr Eyjólfsson, Nedelina Ivanova, Christèle Maizonniaux, Neasa Ní Chiaráin, Manny Rayner, John Sloan, Sigurður Vigfússon and Ghil'ad Zuckermann

10:30–11:00 **coffee break**

11:00–12:00 **Oral presentation**

11:00–11:30 *Agree to Disagree: Exploring Subjectivity in Lexical Complexity*
Matthew Shardlow

11:30–12:00 *A Dictionary-Based Study of Word Sense Difficulty*
David Alfter, Rémi Cardon and Thomas François

Friday, June 24, 2022 (continued)

12:00–13:00 Poster session

13:00–14:00 Lunch break

Friday, June 24, 2022 (continued)

14:10–15:00 Invited speaker

14:10–15:00 *Tools & services for text adaptation*
Arne Jonson

15:00–16:00 READI 2020 presentations

15:00–15:20 *Text Simplification to Help Individuals with Low Vision Read More Fluently*
Lauren Sauvan, Natacha Stolowy, Carlos Aguilar, Thomas François, Núria Gala, Frédéric Matonti, Eric Castet and Aurélie Calabrèse

15:20–15:40 *Disambiguating Confusion Sets as an Aid for Dyslexic Spelling*
Steinunn Rut riðriksdóttir a and Anton Karl Ingason

15:40–16:00 *Incorporating Multiword Expressions in Phrase Complexity Estimation*
Sian Gooding, Shiva Taslimipoor and Ekaterina Kochmar

16:00–16:30 Coffee break

16:30–17:00 Round table: future directions & projects

17:00–17:15 End session

Proceedings of the 2nd READI Workshop @ LREC2022, pages 1–8
Marseille, 24 June 2022

Reading Assistance through LARA, the Learning And Reading Assistant

Elham Akhlaghi[1], Ingibjörg Iða Auðunardóttir[2], Branislav Bédi[3], Hakeem Beedar[4], Harald Berthelsen[5], Cathy Chua[6], Catia Cucchiarini[7], Brynjarr Eyjólfsson[2], Nedelina Ivanova[8], Christèle Maizonniaux[9], Neasa Ní Chiaráin[5], Manny Rayner[10], John Sloan[5,10], Sigurður Vigfússon[8], Ghil'ad Zuckermann[4]
[1]Ferdowsi University of Mashhad, Iran; [2]University of Iceland, Iceland;
[3]The Árni Magnússon Institute for Icelandic Studies, Iceland;
[4]University of Adelaide, Australia; [5]Trinity College, Dublin, Ireland; [6]Independent scholar;
[7]CLST, Radboud University Nijmegen, The Netherlands;
[8]The Communication Centre for the Deaf and Hard of Hearing, Iceland;
[9]Flinders University, Adelaide, Australia; [10]FTI/TIM, University of Geneva, Switzerland;
elhamakhlaghi80@gmail.com, iia2@hi.is, branislav.bedi@arnastofnun.is,
hbeedar@hotmail.com.au, berthelh@tcd.ie, cathyc@pioneerbooks.com.au,
c.cucchiarini@let.ru.nl, jcy1@hi.is, nedelina@shh.is, christele.maizonniaux@flinders.edu.au,
Neasa.NiChiarain@tcd.ie, Emmanuel.Rayner@unige.ch, sloanjo@tcd.ie,
siggivig@gmail.com, ghilad.zuckermann@adelaide.edu.au,

Abstract

We present an overview of LARA, the Learning And Reading Assistant, an open source platform for easy creation and use of multimedia annotated texts designed to support the improvement of reading skills. The paper is divided into three parts. In the first, we give a brief summary of LARA's processing. In the second, we describe some generic functionality specially relevant for reading assistance: support for phonetically annotated texts, support for image-based texts, and integrated production of text-to-speech (TTS) generated audio. In the third, we outline some of the larger projects so far carried out with LARA, involving development of content for learning second and foreign (L2) languages such as Icelandic, Farsi, Irish, Old Norse and the Australian Aboriginal language Barngarla, where the issues involved overlap with those that arise when trying to help students improve first-language (L1) reading skills. All software and almost all content is freely available.

Keywords: CALL, multimodality, reading, open source, evaluation

1. Introduction and overview

LARA (`https://www.unige.ch/callector/lara/`) is an open source learning-by-reading platform under development by an international consortium since 2018. Starting at the University of Geneva, the user base has grown quickly and now includes groups in over a dozen countries. LARA supports easy construction of annotated multimodal texts using open source tools which can either be invoked from the command-line or, more commonly, through an online portal. These texts typically include various features for reading assistance such as integrated audio, translations, and an automatically generated concordance. A screenshot showing a page from a LARA text is shown in Figure 1.

The basic idea of adding multimedia annotations to texts in order to help non-L1 language learners is natural, and has been implemented in some form in many other platforms; prominent examples include LingQ[1], Learning With Texts[2], the Perseus Digital Library's Scaife viewer[3] and Clilstore[4]. What primarily distinguishes LARA from these is the project's open source nature, where new features are added in a bottom-up process driven by the demands of a diverse community involved in many different kinds of language-related projects.

As noted, LARA has originally been developed to help people learn and read non-L1 languages. However, the boundary between non-L1 and L1 turns out to be less clear than we had initially expected. For example, looking ahead to §4.1., a major hurdle for beginner learners of Irish is the opaque writing system, which makes it unusually difficult to acquire a good understanding of the letter/sound rules. The problems these people face are not dissimilar to those experienced by people with L1 reading difficulties. In addition, recent extensions to the LARA functionality are moving in a direction that could make it more directly useful as a tool for providing assistance to people with reading difficulties.

This paper is intended to provide a self-contained overview of the reading assistance facilities in LARA that may be relevant to the reading difficulties community. We start by presenting a brief summary of the core LARA functionality (§2.), then describe recently added functionality particularly relevant in the present context (§3.). In §4. we describe some LARA projects where the issues would appear to overlap with those arising when helping people with reading difficulties. The final section summarises and looks ahead.

2. Core LARA functionality

The core of LARA is a set of tools that make it easy to convert text into the multimodal annotated form illustrated in Figure 1. The conversion process consists of the following

[1]`https://www.lingq.com/`
[2]`https://sourceforge.net/projects/lwt/`
[3]`https://scaife.perseus.org/`
[4]`http://multidict.net/clilstore/`

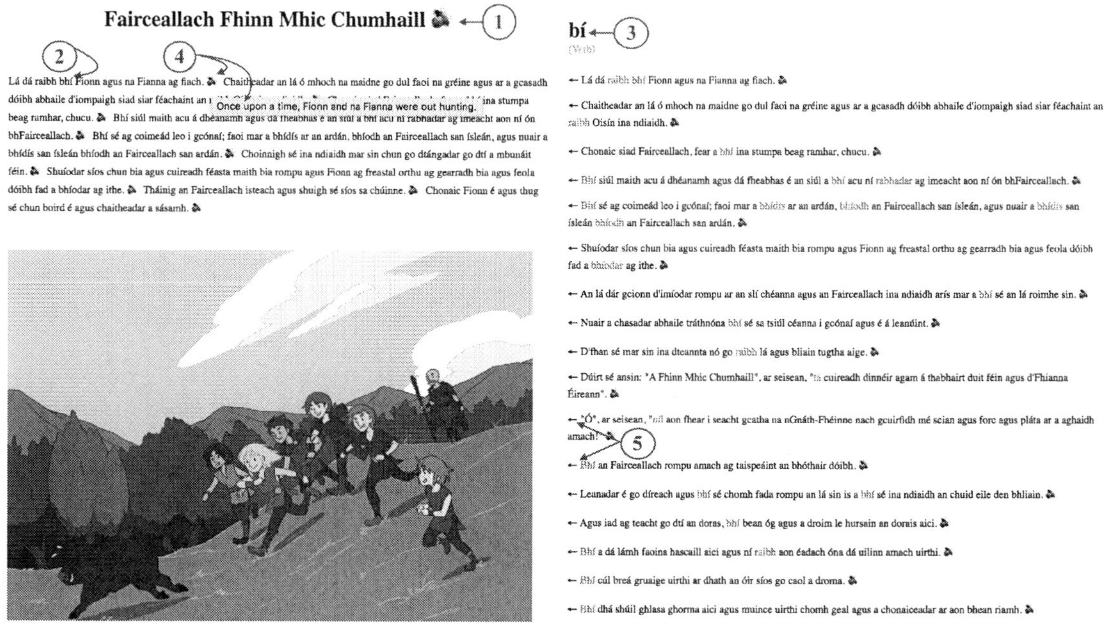

Figure 1: Example of Irish LARA content, *Fairceallach Fhinn Mhic Cumhaill*, ('Fionn's burly friend'), reproduced from (Zuckerman et al., 2021). A 'play all' audio button function is included at the top of the page to enable the listener to hear the entire story in one go (1). The text and images are in the pane on the left hand side. Clicking on a word displays information about it in the right hand pane. Here, the user has clicked on *bhí* = "to be (past tense)" (2), showing an automatically generated concordance; the lemma *bí*; and every variation of *bí* that is in this text (3). Hovering the mouse over a word plays audio and shows a popup translation at word-level. Clicking on a loudspeaker plays audio for the entire sentence as well as showing a popup translation (4). The back-arrows (5) link each line in the concordance to its context of occurrence. A link to the document can be found on the LARA examples page.[6]

steps:

Segment: Segment the text. For European languages, this means splitting up lists of words into sentence-length segments using a sentence tokeniser. The result is then in general manually post-edited.

Tag: Tag the text, to mark each word with its lemma form and (optionally) part of speech. This is needed in order to build the lemma-oriented concordance. When a tagger/lemmatiser is available, this is first used to perform the tagging automatically, after which the result is again manually post-edited. Several tagger/lemmatisers are now integrated into LARA, covering over 20 languages.

Identify resources needed: Process the text to create a set of resource files which specify other annotation data that needs to be added. The most important are i) associations of words and segments with audio files, ii) associations of words and segments with translations, and iii) potential occurrences of multiword expressions (MWEs) taken from an MWE lexicon for the language in question.

Instantiate resources: Upload the resource files to tools which support easy entry of the missing information. Audio files are created through a user-friendly online recording tool. Translations are entered through a spreadsheet-like interface. Candidate MWEs are confirmed or rejected through another interactive tool.

Create pages: Combine all the information to create the multimedia pages.

These operation can either be carried out directly using command-line tools, or can be invoked through the LARA portal, a free online service that provides a user-friendly wizard-style interface. Full details and examples can be found in the online documentation[7].

3. Functionality

We describe three pieces of LARA functionality introduced over the last year that are potentially relevant to helping people with reading difficulties: phonetic texts, annotated images and picture lexica, and integrated TTS.

3.1. Reading assistance through phonetic texts

LARA documents were originally conceived as texts with a hierarchical structure consisting of pages, segments and words, where the words are associated with lemmas. In order to address the needs of students who are uncertain

[7] https://www.issco.unige.ch/en/research/projects/callector/LARADoc/build/html/index.html

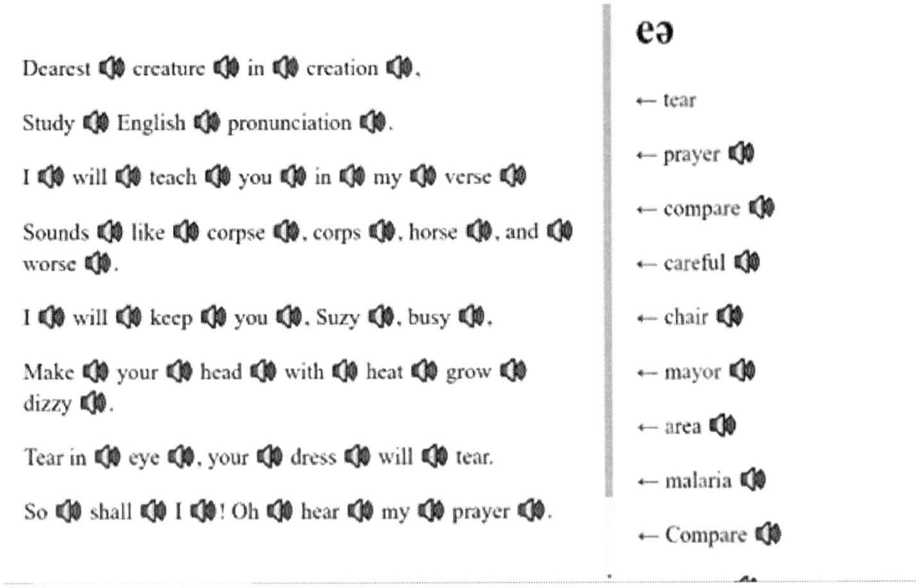

Figure 2: "Phonetic" LARA version of Charivarius's 1920 pronunciation poem *The Chaos* (screenshot of first page). Clicking on a letter group, here "ear" in "tear" at the end of the penultimate line, highlights the group, plays the sound, and shows a phonetic concordance on the right; clicking on a speaker icon plays audio for whole of the preceding word. A link to the text is posted on the LARA examples page.

about letter/sound correspondences, we have recently extended the framework to allow the option of creating texts annotated at the phonetic level. A "phonetic" LARA text is hierarchically divided into pages, words and letter-groups, where each letter-group is associated with a phonetic value. The same notation is used for both types of text, and nearly all of the processing associated with normal (word-oriented) LARA texts carries over to phonetic texts; in particular, a compiled phonetic text contains a phonetic concordance, giving examples of contexts where each phonetic value occurs. A playful example illustrating the "phonetic text" functionality is shown in Figure 2.

It would be extremely laborious to construct phonetic LARA texts by hand, and there is a script that converts a normal text into the corresponding phonetic version. This post-processes the internalised text to convert each word into a corresponding phonetic version, while keeping formatting unchanged. For languages which are written completely phonetically, this only requires the annotator to supply the list of phonetically meaningful letter groups defining the orthography of the language. An example for Barngarla (cf. §4.2.) is *Mangiri Yarda*; this also uses the annotated image functionality described in §3.2..

For languages where online phonetic lexica exist, phonetic versions of most words can be read off the lexicon; free phonetic lexica for many languages are for example available from the IPA-dict project.[8] The challenge is to align the letters with the phonetic symbols. At the moment, the conversion script helps the annotator compile an aligned phonetic lexicon, where typical entries are as illustrated in Figure 4. The script creates new entries automatically using a simple dynamic programming method which maximises the number of alignments already seen in the lexicon (this idea is partly inspired by the one from (Jiampojamarn and Kondrak, 2010)), after which a human annotator cleans up the result. Further details are given in the online documentation.[9]

Once a reasonable number of examples of aligned words have been collected, error rates become low and the cleaning-up process is quick. We present the results of a preliminary evaluation for English and French to support this claim. In English, we began by constructing an initial aligned word lexicon for a few small texts, the largest of which was "The Chaos" (cf. Figure 2). This produced a total of 990 aligned words, which included 264 unique primitive grapheme-sequence/phoneme-sequence correspondences; phonetic transcriptions were taken from the UK English IPA-dict resource. We then ran the alignment guessing script on the text of an English translation of Saint-Exupèry's *Le Petit Prince*. This contained 1833 unique words, of which 309 were already in the aligned-word lexicon. Of the remaining 1524, 78 were not in the IPA-dict lexicon, most of them either because they were heteronyms ("close", "live", "wind") or proper names ("africa", "antoine", "siberia").

Editing the aligned lexicon took an expert annotator, one of the authors, about three hours. Comparing the edited and raw versions, we found that the script had correctly aligned 1410/1524 of the new words (92.5%) and 9041/9580 of the

[8] https://github.com/open-dict-data/ipa-dict

[9] https://www.issco.unige.ch/en/research/projects/callector/LARADoc/build/html/phonetic_texts.html

(a)

```
<annotated_image>
<img src="restaurant_date.jpg" width="800" height="800"/>
chair man glass ||
table ||
glass woman chair ||
</annotated_image>
```

(b)

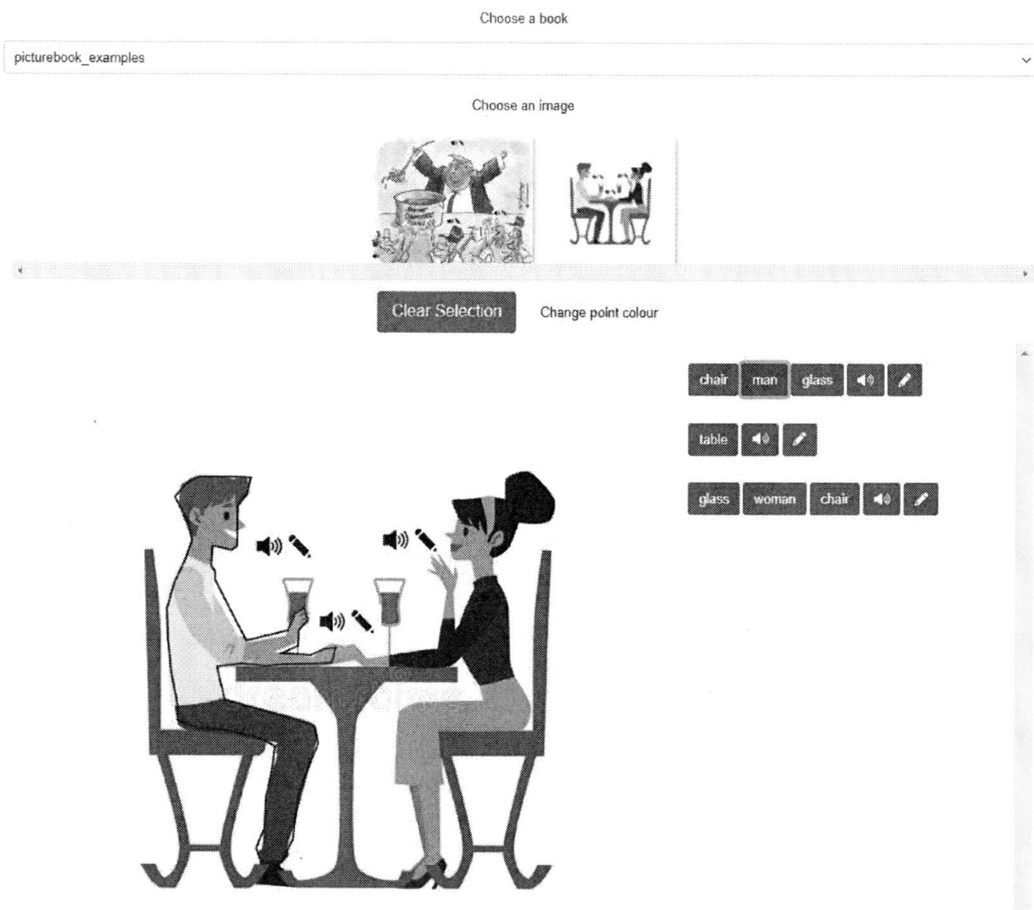

Figure 3: Toy example of a piece of image-based text based on a simple cartoon, taken from (Bédi et al., 2022). The LARA source (a) is given above. The screenshot below (b) shows the tool used to create the word locations file. The top control allows the annotator to choose the text to annotate, after which the slider with the series of thumbnails allows them to choose a page by its image. The bottom left pane presents the selected image, and the bottom right pane the associated words. The annotator can draw a polygon on the left and save it to a word, or select a word on the right to show the current polygon. Here, the annotator has just selected the word "man" on the right, showing the polygon for the picture of the man on the left. The speaker and pencil icons optionally associate audio or text with a whole line. A link to the LARA document is posted on the LARA examples page under "Two cartoons".

graphemes (94.4%). Looking only at the subset for which IPA-dict entries were available, the figures were 1410/1446 (97.5%) for words and 9041/9102 (99.3%) for characters. Audio for the phonetic content was recorded by one of the authors, a native speaker of English.

The French experiment was similar, though the initial version of the aligned lexicon was based on a smaller sample of language. This time, we used the original French edition of *Le Petit Prince* as the evaluation text. This contained 2583 unique words, of which 559 were already in the aligned-word lexicon. Of the remaining 2024, 32 were not in the IPA-dict lexicon. Again, editing the guessed aligned lexicon took about three hours. The script correctly aligned 1876/2024 of the new words (92.7%) and 13722/14191 of the graphemes (96.7%). For the subset where IPA-dict entries were available, the figures were 1876/1992 (94.2%) and 13722/13966 (98.3%) for graphemes. This time, we experimented with a different strategy for creating the phonetic audio, and generated it using one of the French voices on the IPA-reader site.[10].

Links to the English and French versions are posted on the LARA examples page under the titles "The Little Prince" and "Le petit prince".

<table>
<tr><td>"admirateur"
"a|d|m|i|r|a|t|eu|r"
"a|d|m|i|ʁ|a|t|œ|ʁ"</td></tr>
<tr><td>"ainsi"
"ain|s|i"
"ɛ̃|s|i|"</td></tr>
<tr><td>"alors"
"a|l|o|r|s"
"a|l|ɔ|ʁ|"</td></tr>
</table>

Figure 4: Examples of entries from French aligned pronunciation lexicon. Several letters can map into one (beginning of "ainsi"), and letters can map into the empty string (end of "alors").

3.2. Annotated images and picture lexica

Another extension to the original text-based LARA document structure concerns images. LARA has always supported inclusion of images using the HTML <img> tag, but these were represented internally as atomic constituents without internal structure. Layout was added using other HTML tags. Although this model works well for many documents, it ignores the fact that a written text is not just a collection of strings but also a visual object. For some kinds of documents, for example picture-books and posters, the visual content can be as important as the words.

In order to address these issues, which are particularly relevant to helping students with reading difficulties, we have recently added new functionality to allow "annotated images" as components of a text. A component of this kind is delimited using the <annotated_image> tag. It must contain exactly one <img> tag and some text, where the text is interpreted as being associated with locations in the image. During the processing phase which identifies resources needed for a text, the images and associated words are extracted, after which they are uploaded to an online graphical tool where the annotator can draw the outline for the location of each word in an image. Figure 3 illustrates. The graphical correlate of a word can, but does not need to be a graphical representation of the word; it can equally well be a part of the image associated with the word. So for example the word "apple" could be associated in the image with the handwritten text *APPLE*, but it could also be associated with an area of the image showing an apple. In the final LARA text, the locations in the image marked as associated with words react to clicking or hovering actions.

Another piece of image-related functionality is the provision of support adding a "picture lexicon" to a text, which associates some lemmas with graphical images. This has already been used for the Barngarla project (cf. §4.2.). The initial text "Welcome to Country with picture lexicon" linked from the examples page was warmly approved by the Barngarla elders guiding the language revival process.

3.3. Reading assistance through integrated TTS

Integration of TTS was primarily implemented to support the Irish group (cf. §4.1.), who have from the start used it exclusively to create Irish language audio. Initially, other groups were sceptical about creating LARA content that used TTS audio, believing that the quality would be insufficient compared to human-recorded audio.

Two collaborative evaluation exercises have however demonstrated that, for many languages, TTS works much better than was generally expected. The first of these exercises was carried out during Q1 2021 and involved the Australian, Icelandic, Iranian, Irish, Dutch, Polish, Slovak and Swiss groups. About twenty LARA documents, in various languages, were produced in both TTS and human audio form and compared by 130 evaluators using an anonymous web form. One expects TTS audio to be much quicker to produce, but of lower quality: the goal was to obtain quantitative and qualitative data exploring the issues. The results were presented at EUROCALL 2021 (Akhlaghi et al., 2021). To our surprise, TTS audio was in fact rated equal to or better than human audio in three of the ten languages. A follow-on study was carried out in Q1 2022 and will be presented at the LREC 2022 conference. Since it used data taken from a uniform text, different translations of Saint-Exupèry's *Le petit prince*, comparisons between languages were more obviously meaningful, and the number of evaluators was approximately doubled. The results were similar to those of the first study. Although the quality of TTS varied widely between languages, the best TTS voices were of a quality comparable with non-professional human voices and again were in some cases preferred.

4. Example projects

LARA was originally designed for creating annotated texts that would improve learners' reading and listening skills in L2 languages. After three years of experience in using the tool, it turns out that the dividing line between L2 and L1 is less clear than we had realised, and that the issues appear to overlap to a considerable extent. We briefly describe some substantial projects exemplifying this observation. In §4.1. we consider the paradoxical case of Irish, where a country's official first language is simultaneously an endangered language. §4.2. describes use of LARA with Barngarla, an Australian Aboriginal language which for several decades was considered dead, but which is now being revived by ethnic Barngarla people. In §4.3. we look at texts designed to help Deaf Icelandic children improve their reading skills in Icelandic, and in §4.4. at Old Norse, the archaic form of Icelandic taught as an obligatory subject in Icelandic schools. §4.5. reviews a project carried out in Iran, where a series of Farsi readers have been converted into LARA form.

[10] http://ipa-reader.xyz/; "Celine" voice.

4.1. Online resources for reading assistance in Irish

Irish is in the possibly unique position of being both the official first language of a sovereign state and also an endangered language. It is a community language only in relatively small regions (Gaeltacht regions) in the West of Ireland, with daily speaker numbers of about 20,000, or less than 0.5% of the Irish population (CSO, 2016). At the same time, it is an obligatory subject in schools, with 700,000 learners in the education system in the Republic of Ireland (Ní Chiaráin and Ní Chasaide, 2020).

Teaching and learning Irish presents multiple challenges, and learning to read Irish is one of them. The first language of most learners will be English, a Germanic language whose structure diverges substantially from that of the Celtic language Irish; the basic word-order of Irish is different (VSO as opposed to English SVO), and it is highly inflected, with up to 42 inflected forms for verbs. A striking feature of the sound system is the contrast of palatalised and velarised consonants, with a very large inventory, relative to English. This feature is partially obscured, and complicated for learners, by the notoriously opaque writing system, and the link of the sounds to written forms is often poorly understood. The initial sounds of lexical items 'mutate' in certain grammatical contexts, so that e.g., in a word like bord 'table' it may be [b], [w], [v] or [m]. Although there is an agreed standardised written form, there is no single spoken standard, but rather three major dialects. Teachers are typically second language learners themselves, and their own confidence in the language can be problematic. They often feel overburdened with the major responsibility placed on them in the revitalisation and maintenance initiative, but report inadequate resources and training to fulfil it (Dunne, 2019).

In this context, it turns out that LARA has much to offer in terms of reading assistance. Using the synthetic voices developed for the main Irish dialects by the ABAIR project (ABAIR, 2020) and integrated into LARA, it is easy to link text to audio in any of the three dialects, bringing a native speaker model directly into the classroom; the lemma-based concordance similarly allows the learner to access the dictionary form of any word with a single click. Starting with pilot LARA adaptations of traditional Irish folkstories, the team at Trinity College Dublin have created a substantial set of Irish reading material in LARA form, posted on the *An Scéalaí* ("The Storyteller") CALL platform.[11]. User feedback has been extremely positive. In a recent survey, for example, 92% of 494 adult respondents reported that using *An Scéalaí* had a positive impact on their language learning journey. 90% of same stated they would like to continue using the platform into the future. Many users commented that LARA made complex texts accessible - learners felt they engaged more deeply and spent more time on 'difficult' reading materials than they would otherwise have done if presented to them in a more traditional format.

4.2. Reading assistance in Barngarla, a revived Australian Aboriginal language

Barngarla is an Australian Aboriginal language belonging to the Thura-Yura language group, a subgroup of the large Pama-Nyungan language family. Typically for a Pama-Nyungan language, Barngarla has a phonemic inventory featuring three vowels ([a], [i], [u]) and retroflex consonants, an ergative grammar with many cases, and a complex pronominal system. Unusual features include a number system with singular, dual, plural and superplural and matrilineal and patrilineal distinction in the dual.
During the twentieth century, Barngarla was intentionally eradicated under Australian 'stolen generation' policies, the last original native speaker dying in 1960. Language reclamation efforts were launched in 2011 (Zuckermann, 2020). Since then, a series of language reclamation workshops have been held in which about 120 Barngarla people have participated. The primary resource used has been a dictionary, including a brief grammar, written by the German Lutheran missionary Clamor Wilhelm Schürmann (Schürmann, 1844; Clendon, 2015).
Other published resources for Barngarla, non-existent ten years ago, are now emerging. The most visible example to date is *Barngarlidhi Manoo* (Zuckermann and the Barngarla, 2019), a Barngarla alphabet book/primer compiled by Ghil'ad Zuckermann in collaboration with the nascent Barngarla revivalistic community. A first step in evaluating the possible relevance of LARA to Barngarla was to convert this book into LARA form (Butterweck et al., 2019). The LARA reading assistance functionality is primarily used to attach audio recordings to Barngarla language: words and phrases marked in red can be played by hovering the mouse over them.
A second resource was produced as part of the "Fifty Words Project"[12], which collects together fifty basic words such as "fire", "water", "sun" and "moon" for several dozen Aboriginal languages. The Barngarla version, recorded by ethnic Barngarla language custodian Jenna Richards from Galinyala (= Port Lincoln), is available on the Fifty Words page. A third Barngarla text, *Mangiri Yarda* ("Healthy Country") (Zuckermann and Richards, 2021) has been designed as a teaching resource. In contrast to *Barngarlidhi Manoo*, which is almost exclusively focused on vocabulary, *Mangiri Yarda* introduces some grammar.
Links to all of these texts are posted on the LARA examples page.

4.3. Helping Deaf Icelanders improve their reading skills

Although Icelandic is the primary language of Iceland, Deaf children usually grow up learning a signed language as their first language. In practice, written Icelandic is not perceived as an L1 for these children, so tools that can help them make progress in reading are potentially very useful.
It turned out to be quite easy to extend LARA so that it can support this kind of scenario: basically, all that was necessary was to arrange things so that recorded signed video can systematically be used as an alternative to recorded au-

[11]`https://abair.ie/scealai/#/landing`

[12]`https://50words.online/`

dio. Thus a LARA text of this type is written in Icelandic, but words and sentences are associated with Icelandic Sign Language (ÍTM) signed videos. The signed video for a word is accessed by clicking on the word; the signed video for a sentence is accessed by clicking on a camera icon inserted at the end of the sentence. (In 'video mode', the camera icon replaces the usual loudspeaker icon).

Videos are recorded using the same third-party recording tool as is used for recording audio content; the tool had already been adapted for this purpose in a previous project (Ahmed et al., 2016). The workflow for recording is modality-independent. The LARA portal creates the recording script from the text and uploads it to the recording tool; the voice talent/signer records the audio/video from the script; at the end, the portal downloads the recorded multimedia and inserts it into the LARA document.

A link to an initial example of a LARA document of this kind, a children's story about 2.7K words long, is posted on the LARA examples page. The student who created the signed content turned to two members of staff at the Center for feedback. One is a native ÍTM signer and the other has worked as an sign language interpreter for over two decades. There were many things to consider, as ÍTM is not a standardised language, even to the extent that the basic word order is unclear: research (Brynjólfsdóttir, 2012) shows that subjects accept both SOV and SVO word orders. The central issue was the question of whether the signed translation of the text should be true to the Icelandic original or re-expressed in ÍTM. One argument is that, as a tool to learn written Icelandic, the translation should be faithful to the source so that ÍTM signs corresponding to the Icelandic words appearing there. The argument in the opposite direction is that a free re-interpretation is better suited to helping Deaf children understand the signed content. In the end an interpreting strategy was preferred for three reasons. Comprehension of the signed text is crucial for Deaf children; the interpreting strategy seemed to be a better fit to the content of a children's book; and in LARA learners can click on a word in the Icelandic text to see the ÍTM sign, if the corresponding sign did not appear in the freely translated segments.

4.4. Assistance in reading Old Norse epic poems

Old Norse, the language spoken in what is now Scandinavia from the 7th to the 15th century, is an important part of Icelandic culture. The linguistic evolution of Icelandic has proceeded more slowly than that of the mainland languages (Danish, Norwegian and Swedish), and it is close enough to Old Norse that Old Norse literary works are still more or less comprehensible; a reasonable comparison point for anglophones might be Chaucerian English. Old Norse language and literature is an obligatory subject in Icelandic secondary schools. It is however clear that many students find it challenging. They are particularly challenged by the Poetic Edda, a classic poem-cycle first written down in the late 13th century, which occupies a central place in the Old Norse canon. The dense, allusive language is much harder to understand than that in prose works, and the less motivated students often experience it as close to incomprehensible.

Particularly as a tagged version of the Poetic Edda already existed, the group at the Árni Magnússon Institute for Icelandic Studies felt that this combination of circumstances made it a good target for conversion into LARA form. Three of the best-known poems from the cycle — the *Völuspá*, *Hávamál* and *Lokasenna* — have now been completed, and several more are in preparation. The *Völuspá* project is presented in (Bédi et al., 2020); as described there, initial feedback from Icelandic users has been very positive. All three of the Eddaic poems so far released have also been used as the basis of reading groups on the popular Goodreads review site.[13]. They attracted a small but enthusiastic audience, with a total of 185 posts for the three groups.

4.5. Online resources for reading assistance in Farsi

The Ferdowsi University of Mashhad (FUM; third highest ranked university in Iran) has used LARA since shortly after the inception of the LARA project. FUM began by developing short LARA texts in Farsi, for use in a Farsi course for Arabic-speaking students at FUM. Early results are reported in (Akhlaghi et al., 2019). This pilot exercise was successful enough that Iranian funding was granted to convert an five-volume series of Farsi textbooks, developed at FUM by Professor Ehsan Ghabool, into LARA form. The project was completed during Q1 2021, and the result is now being used at FUM's International Center for Teaching Persian to Non-Persian People[14].

5. Summary and further directions

We have presented a brief overview of the LARA community and platform, focusing on issues that overlap with those relevant to supporting people with reading difficulties and illustrating with some practical use cases. Work in several of these areas is under active development. We are particularly interested in exploring the possibilities opened up by the new "phonetic text" and "annotated image" functionalities, and welcome suggestions from the reading difficulties community about ways to repurpose the LARA technology to this new domain.

6. Bibliographical References

ABAIR, (2020). *ABAIR: An Sintéiseoir Gaeilge - The Irish Language Synthesiser ABAIR.* http://www.abair.ie. As of 8 September 2020.

Ahmed, F., Bouillon, P., Destefano, C., Gerlach, J., Hooper, A., Rayner, M., Strasly, I., Tsourakis, N., and Weiss, C. (2016). Rapid construction of a web-enabled medical speech to sign language translator using recorded video. In *Proceedings of FETLT 2016*, Seville, Spain.

[13] https://www.goodreads.com/topic/show/21221144-v-lusp-reading-group-verses-1-6; https://www.goodreads.com/topic/show/22046862-h-vam-l-reading-group; https://www.goodreads.com/topic/show/22089678-lokasenna-reading-group

[14] 2 100 students; https://ctpl.um.ac.ir/index.php?lang=en

Akhlaghi, E., Bédi, B., Butterweck, M., Chua, C., Gerlach, J., Habibi, H., Ikeda, J., Rayner, M., Sestigiani, S., and Zuckermann, G. (2019). Overview of LARA: A learning and reading assistant. In *Proc. SLaTE 2019: 8th ISCA Workshop on Speech and Language Technology in Education*, pages 99–103.

Akhlaghi, E., Bączkowska, A., Berthelsen, H., Bédi, B., Chua, C., Cuchiarini, C., Habibi, H., Horváthová, I., Hvalsøe, P., Lotz, R., Maizonniaux, C., Ní Chiaráin, N., Rayner, M., Tsourakis, N., and Yao, C. (2021). Assessing the quality of TTS audio in the LARA learning-by-reading platform. In N. Zoghlami, et al., editors, *CALL and professionalisation: short papers from EUROCALL 2021*, pages 1–5.

Bédi, B., Bernharðsson, H., Chua, C., Guðmarsdóttir, B. B., Habibi, H., and Rayner, M. (2020). Constructing an interactive old norse text with lara. *CALL for widening participation: short papers from EUROCALL*, pages 27–35.

Brynjólfsdóttir, E. G. (2012). *Hvað gerðir þú við peningana sem frúin í Hamborg gaf þér? Myndun hv-spurninga í íslenska táknmálinu.* Ph.D. thesis.

Butterweck, M., Chua, C., Habibi, H., Rayner, M., and Zuckermann, G. (2019). Easy construction of multimedia online language textbooks and linguistics papers with LARA. In *Proc. 12th annual International Conference of Education, Research and Innovation*, Seville, Spain.

Bédi, B., Beedar, H., Chiera, B., Ivanova, N., Maizonniaux, C., Chiaráin, N. N., Rayner, M., Sloan, J., and Zuckermann, G. (2022). Using lara to create image-based and phonetically annotated multimodal texts for endangered languages. In *Proceedings of the Workshop on Computational Methods for Endangered Languages*.

Clendon, M. (2015). *Clamor Schürmann's Barngarla grammar: A commentary on the first section of A vocabulary of the Parnkalla language*. University of Adelaide Press.

CSO, (2016). *Census 2016 Profile 10 – Education, Skills and the Irish Language.* https://www.cso.ie/en/csolatestnews/presspages/2017. As of 11 October 2020.

Dunne, C. M. (2019). Primary teachers' experiences in preparing to teach Irish: Views on promoting the language and language proficiency. *Studies in Self-Access Learning*, 10(1):21–43.

Jiampojamarn, S. and Kondrak, G. (2010). Letter-phoneme alignment: An exploration. In *Proceedings of the 48th Annual Meeting of the Association for Computational Linguistics, Uppsala, Sweden*, pages 780–788.

Ní Chiaráin, N. and Ní Chasaide, A. (2020). The potential of text-to-speech synthesis in computer-assisted language learning: A minority language perspective. In Alberto Andujar, editor, *Recent Tools for Computer- and Mobile-Assisted Foreign Language Learning*, chapter 7, pages 149–169. IGI Global, Hershey, PA.

Schürmann, C. W. (1844). *A Vocabulary of the Parnkalla Language. Spoken by the natives inhabiting the western shore of Spencer's Gulf. To which is prefixed a collection of grammatical rules, hitherto ascertained.*

Zuckerman, G., Vigfússon, S., Rayner, M., Chiaráin, N. N., Ivanova, N., Habibi, H., and Bédi, B. (2021). Lara in the service of revivalistics and documentary linguistics: Community engagement and endangered languages. In *Proceedings of the Workshop on Computational Methods for Endangered Languages*, volume 1, pages 13–23.

Zuckermann, G. and Richards, E. (2021). *Mangiri Yarda (Healthy Country: Barngarla Wellbeing and Nature).* Revivalistics Press.

Zuckermann, G. and the Barngarla. (2019). *Barngarlidhi Manoo: "Speaking Barngarla Together".* Barngarla Language Advisory Committee (BLAC).

Zuckermann, G. (2020). *Revivalistics: From the Genesis of Israeli to Language Reclamation in Australia and Beyond.* New York: Oxford University Press.

Proceedings of the 2nd READI Workshop @ LREC2022, pages 9–16
Marseille, 24 June 2022

Agree to Disagree: Exploring Subjectivity in Lexical Complexity

Matthew Shardlow
Manchester Metropolitan University
M.Shardlow@mmu.ac.uk

Abstract

Subjective factors affect our familiarity with different words. Our education, mother tongue, dialect or social group all contribute to the words we know and understand. When asking people to mark words they understand some words are unanimously agreed to be complex, whereas other annotators universally disagree on the complexity of other words. In this work, we seek to expose this phenomenon and investigate the factors affecting whether a word is likely to be subjective, or not. We investigate two recent word complexity datasets from shared tasks. We demonstrate that subjectivity is present and describable in both datasets. Further we show results of modelling and predicting the subjectivity of the complexity annotations in the most recent dataset, attaining an F1-score of 0.714.

Keywords: Complex Word Identification, Lexical Complexity Prediction, Text Simplification

1. Introduction

Lexical Complexity Prediction (LCP) has applications in Text Simplification (Zampieri et al., 2017), as well as Readability Assessment (Ehara, 2020). It is the task of identifying how complex a word is likely to be for an end user. Similarly, Complex Word Identification (CWI) is the task of identifying whether a word is complex or not. In both these tasks, disagreements naturally arise between annotators seeking to faithfully give their subjective opinions on the difficulty of the words in question. Take, for example the following sentence, taken from the CWI2018 shared task data (Yimam et al., 2017):

> "A man and a woman questioned on suspicion of assisting an **offender** have been released."

The marked token (*offender*) may be considered complex by some and simple by others. In fact this example split the pool of annotators, being marked complex by 50% of the annotators and simple by the rest. This is not always the case though, and there are also words that are consistently annotated. For example, in the LCP2021 data (Shardlow et al., 2022), the following example is given:

> "Similarly, changes in **synaptic plasticity** due to Ca2+-permeable AMPARs [51,52,60], e.g., in piriform cortex, might alter odor memorization processes."

Clearly, here the entire context is very hard to understand, and the term in that context (*synaptic plasticity*) is inaccessible to a non-domain expert. As such, the term was annotated as the highest level of difficulty by all but one annotator.

Similarly, in the following context, also taken from LCP2021 all annotators chose the easiest level of difficulty for the token *hand*:

> "But he, beckoning to them with his **hand** to be silent, declared to them how the Lord had brought him out of the prison."

We can draw from these few examples that there are clear cases where annotators agree, and clear cases where annotators do not agree. These exist across multiple datasets and are not merely a factor of the token's complexity (i.e., we may naïvely assume that everyone agrees on simple words, but differs on complex words, or vice versa). For sake of ease, we will refer to *subjectivity* in the remainder of this paper in the context of the subjectivity of complexity.

These initial insights allow us to form the following research hypotheses and questions:

RQ1: Can we distinguish words with subjective or consistent complexity? Are they the same across different datasets?

- **RH1.1:** We can identify from existing datasets clear patterns of subjective and non-subjective complexity annotations.
- **RH1.2** The subjective and non-subjective complex words will be the same across datasets.

RQ2: What factors model subjectivity?

- **RH2.1:** Lexical ambiguity will correlate to subjectivity.
- **RH2.2:** Lexical frequency will correlate to subjectivity.
- **RH2.3:** Psycholinguistic norms will correlate to subjectivity.

RQ3: Can we reliably predict which words are likely to be consistently annotated as complex or simple, and which words are likely to be subjectively complex?

- **RH3.1:** Classical machine learning classifiers can predict subjectivity based on the lexical factors identified.

To answer these questions, the remainder of the paper is structured as follows: We define the notions of complexity and subjectivity in Section 2 and explore this in a concrete manner in Sections 3 and 4, which cover datasets from two shared tasks. We also discuss the internal mechanisms that were used during annotation and demonstrate the subjectivity that is present, which addresses RH1.1. Section 5 compares the two datasets in terms of the words that are found to be consistent or subjective and addresses RH1.2 accordingly. Section 6 identifies a number of pertinent features taken from the CWI/LCP literature and uses statistical methods to determine their relation to the subjectivity, addressing RH2.1–3. We build various classifiers to predict subjectivity in Section 7, which allows us to answer RH3.1. The paper concludes with a discussion of the work (Section 8) and a short discussion of the limited related works that exist (Section 9).

2. Definitions

We make an initial definition of the notion of subjectivity as follows. We build on this definition in the context of two datasets in Sections 3 and 4.

> The complexity of a word is considered *subjective* if the returned complexity labels for that word span a range of complexity values.

More formally, we can define a complexity annotation scheme as taking vocabulary items v_i from some vocabulary V and presenting them to a discrete set of n human annotators $h_1, ..., h_n$, drawn from a pool H of size at least n who each return some label l drawn from a discrete ordinal integer label set L. An annotation a_i can be defined as a point in the relation $A = H \times L$ and each v_i receives n annotations which can be represented as a vector $\vec{a}$ (with indices $a_1 ... a_n$). Given these conditions, we can define 2 properties, complexity and subjectivity as follows. The complexity of a vocabulary item v_i is the mean of the ordinal values of the labels in the annotations:

$$Complexity(v_i) = \frac{\sum_{j=1}^{N} a_j}{n} \tag{1}$$

Similarly, we can use these definitions to define a formal measure of subjectivity modelled on the average absolute deviation of $\vec{a}$:

$$Subjectivity(v_i) = \frac{\sum_{j=1}^{n} |Complexity(v_i) - a_j|}{n} \tag{2}$$

We may also define thresholds for complexity T_c and subjectivity T_s by which we define a vocabulary item as holding the property of complex or subjective:

$$Complex(v_i) \rightarrow Complexity(v_i) > T_c \tag{3}$$

$$Subjective(v_i) \rightarrow Subjectivity(v_i) > T_s \tag{4}$$

T_c may be sensibly set at 0.5 in complexity research, although this could be varied depending on the requirements of an application. T_s will be some function of the magnitude of L (i.e., the more categories to choose from, the wider deviation is acceptable before crossing the subjectivity threshold) and also of N (i.e., the more annotators that we have, the more potential for subjectivity). We propose the following definition for determining a subjectivity threshold as follows:

$$T_s = \alpha \times |L| \times n \tag{5}$$

where α is a normalising constant set to some small value between 0 and 1. We report on empirical values of α in the next two sections.

3. Subjectivity in CWI2018 Annotations

The CWI2018 data covered Wiki text and Newswire data. Annotators were asked to identify any word or span that they found to be complex in a context. Each context was presented to 20 annotators, of which 10 were native speakers of English and 10 were not. This resulted in 20 binary annotations for each identified term which indicated whether an annotator considered that term complex. These binary annotations were represented by the ordinal labels 0 and 1 such that if every annotator agreed a word was complex it would have 20 positive annotations and get a score of 1. If no annotator considered a word complex it would have 20 zeroes and be given an overall score of 0.

Interestingly from the point of view of subjectivity, annotator disagreement is directly modelled in the complexity labels. As in the initial example given in the introduction, if 10 annotators found a word to be complex, whereas 10 found it to be simple, the word would be given a score of 0.5, according to the formulae given in Section 2.

We investigate the nature of subjectivity in the English portion of CWI2018 data through the 3 plots in Figure 1. We firstly show in Figure 1a the distribution of subjectivity values in the CWI2018 dataset. These values were calculated using the formula for subjectivity given above. It is clear that most items in the dataset fall in the lower end of the subjectivity — coming in the 0.0–0.1 bin. These represent both complex and simple words, although the majority are simple words due to the nature of the dataset. There are a number of words in the subsequent bands, with the highest bin (0.4–0.5) having just under 3000 examples. Figure 1b shows the relationship between subjectivity and complexity in the binary annotation setting of CWI2018. The bell curve that arises represents the fact that the lowest-subjective elements are those with high or low complexity (everyone agreed either way), whereas the most subjective elements are those with a mid-level complexity (half the annotators said simple, the other half said complex). Finally, Figure 1c shows the effect of varying alpha (And hence the threshold) on the proportion of words

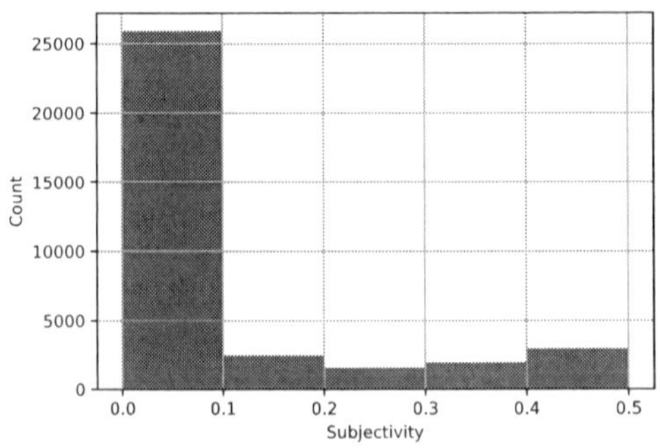

(a) A histogram showing the distribution of the subjectivity values in the CWI2018 data. Whilst most data is of low-subjectivity. There are clear examples on the right of the graph where annotators disagreed.

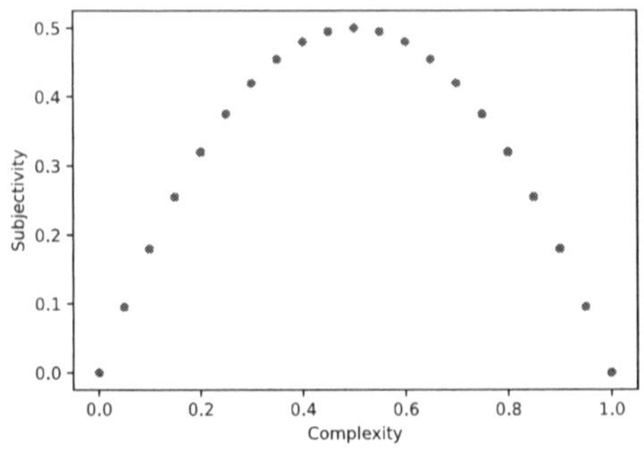

(b) Subjectivity vs. complexity. The bell curve arises due to the binary annotation scheme as described in Section 3.

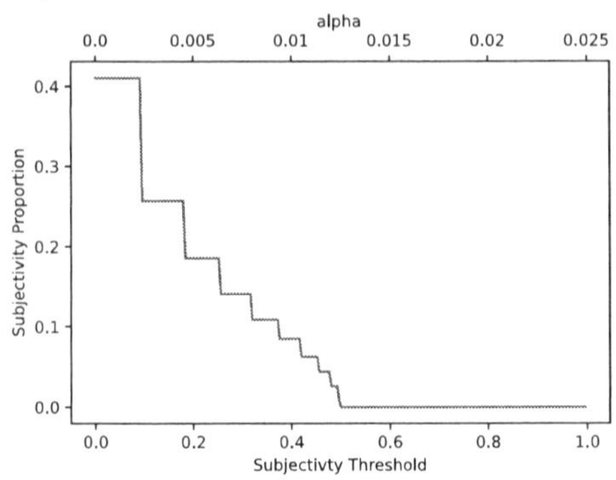

(c) The result of varying the subjectivity threshold according to α. Around 40% of the instances are considered subjective at low values of α.

Figure 1: Analysis of the subjectivity values in the CWI2018 dataset annotations.

that are considered subjective. A subjectivity threshold above 0.5 ($\alpha = 0.0125$) leads to no words being considered subjective. Figure 1c demonstrates that the subjectivity threshold can be empirically set to determine the words that are determined as subjective. A subjectivity threshold of 0.4 ($\alpha = 0.01$) would result in 5% of instances being considered subjective, whereas a lower threshold of 0.2 ($\alpha = 0.005$) would result in 15% of instances considered subjective. A few examples of words across subjectivity values are described in Table 1.

Subj	Terms
0.0	back, bomb, censorship, death, instilled
0.25	assets, cushion, launches, previously
0.5	approaching, credence, overspending, slash

Table 1: Terms by subjectivity for CWI2018

We can see from Table 1 that both simple (back, town) and complex (censorship, instilled) terms were agreed upon by all annotators. The most controversial words are typically longer words that may require some subjective or domain knowledge to fully understand.

4. Subjectivity in LCP2021 Annotations

Whereas the CWI2018 data used binary annotation ($L = \{0, 1\}$) the LCP2021 task used a 5-point Likert scale ($L = \{0, 1, 2, 3, 4\}$). This allows annotators to agree on points in the Likert scale that do not represent the poles of the scale. For example, annotators may all agree that an instance is of medium complexity with a subjectivity of 0. Equally, annotators may nearly agree, centering around a given point, but disagreeing (within varying margins) from that point. Finally, it is possible that an instance might polarise the annotator pool. For example, if an instance is ambiguous one set of annotators may interpret in one way, whereas another take another interpretation. The first interpretation might lead to annotations of simplicity, whereas the latter leads to annotations of difficulty — creating a multi-modal distribution in the returned annotations. This has some negative ramifications for the definition of complexity used in this work, as the mean implicitly assumes a normal distribution. The complexity is still reflective of a central point in the annotations, but not a maximal point in this scenario. However, for our definition of subjectivity, the case of multi-modal distributions will still lead to high subjectivity values as the multiple modes will be separated from the centralised complexity value. In any case, this may become more of an issue with continuous annotations, as opposed to a 5-point Likert scale, where the few points in the scale force annotator decisions around common poles.

To investigate the phenomenon of subjectivity in the LCP2021 data, we applied the same transform following the equations from Section 2 to the original annotations to give a complexity and subjectivity value for each instance. The number of annotations for each instance in the LCP2021 data is 10. We demonstrate the subjectivity of these annotations by creating the same figures as for the CWI2018 data, as shown in Figure 2. Figure 2a demonstrates the distribution of subjectivity values in our dataset, with a mean around 0.6 and subjectivity ranging from 0 to 1.5. (N.b., subjectivity is

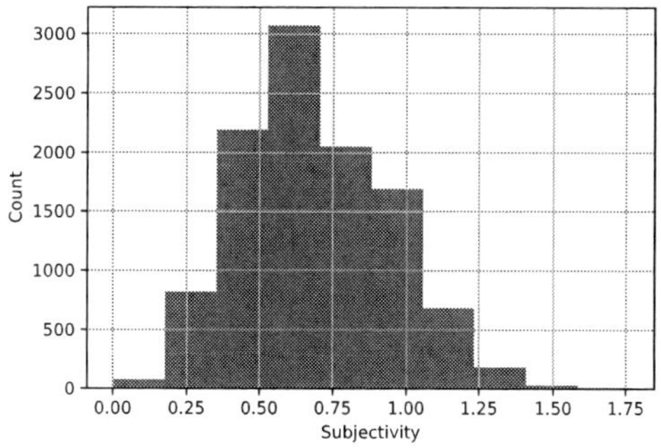

(a) A histogram showing the distribution of the subjectivity values in the LCP2021 data.

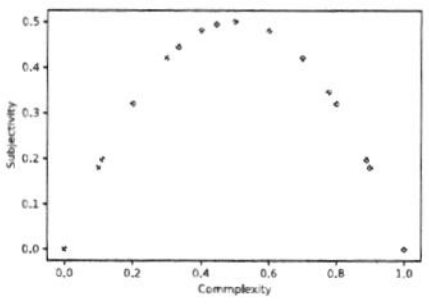

(b) Subjectivity vs. complexity with 2 labels.

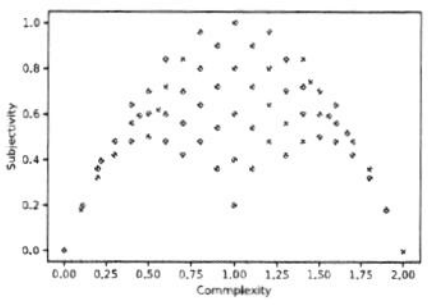

(c) Subjectivity vs. complexity with 3 labels.

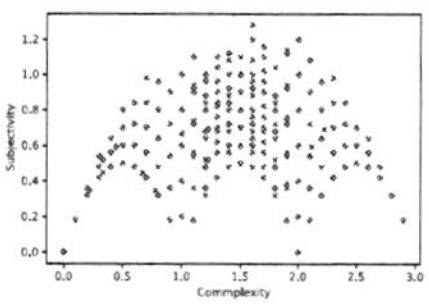

(d) Subjectivity vs. complexity with 4 labels.

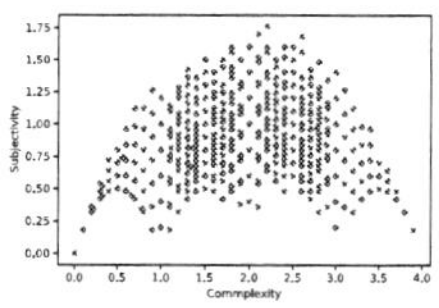

(e) Subjectivity vs. complexity with 5 labels.

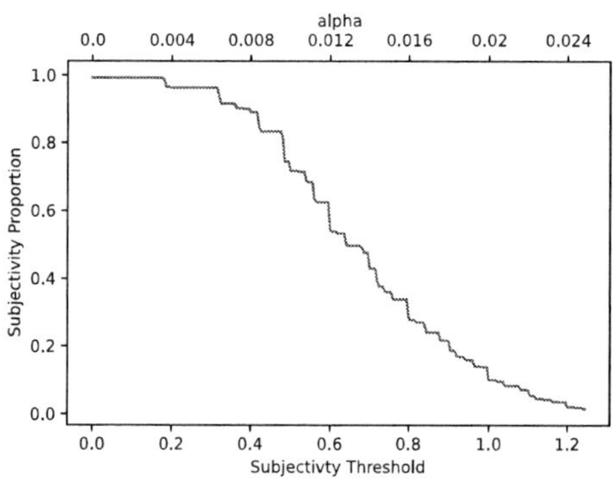

(f) The result of varying the subjectivity threshold according to α.

Figure 2: Analysis of the subjectivity values in the LCP2018 dataset annotations.

not capped at 1 as it is a function of the ordinal labels which range from 0-4). The distribution appears to be Gaussian, with a left skew. The range of the values can be interpreted in the context of the number of labels available. A subjectivity of 0.6 means that the annotations were within 0.6 points of a label of each other. The maximum possible subjectivity in a 5-label annotation setting would be where an equal number of annotators have selected polarised values. (i.e., 0 and 4). In this case, the complexity of the annotations for any N would be 2, as would the subjectivity. So a subjectivity of 1.0 in this setting is half of the theoretical maximum possible subjectivity. Almost all of the annotations fall below this mark.

To further investigate the effect that the number of annotators has on the distribution of the annotation with respect to complexity, we first recast the 5-point scale as a binary annotation. We further recast the problem as a 3 and 4 point annotation problem by relabelling in the manner described in Table 2, where the top row describes the original annotation point and the subsequent describe the transformed point. [1] Applying the transform allowed us to produce the graphs in Figures 2b–2e.

Original	0	1	2	3	4
2-label	0	0	1	1	1
3-label	0	0	1	2	2
4-label	0	1	2	2	3

Table 2: Label transforms used.

To describe the boundaries of the graphs in Figures 2b–2e, we can consider that the y-axis is determined by the complexity and the x-axis is determined by the subjectivity. In the simplest case (Figure 2b) a parabola is formed as the subjectivity requires the complexity to be calculated, summing the number of instances once to calculate the mean and then again to calculate the subjectivity (hence x^2). It is logical to consider that when we have only labels 0 and 1, the subjectivity will be 0 when the complexity is 0 and the subjectivity will be 1 when the complexity is 1 (as these cases can both only arise when the vector is all zeroes, or all ones). Similarly, when the complexity is 0.5, the subjectivity is also 0.5 as this arises when the annotator pool is perfectly polarised (i.e., half have chosen zero and half have chosen one).

Let us then consider the more complex case of Figure 2c. In this graph there are 3 labels available to the annotators. We can see that the annotations fall in a space that can be described by three boundaries. The upper boundary is described as above, the case where the annotation vector contains only instances of 0 or 2 (2 being the largest possible annotation). It is the same curve as in Figure 2b, but is twice as high and twice as wide. There are also two clear lower bounds in the graph. The first, between 0 and 1 on the x-axis is described by the curve in Figure 2b as it is the case of annotations which contain only zeroes and ones (i.e., no twos). The second, falling between one and two on the x-axis is

[1] The relabelling is done in arbitrary manner to enable us to investigate the same effect in the 2, 3 and 4 point setting. It is not intended as a robust means of reducing the number of labels in an annotation setting.

described by a new curve, which is the same shape as the other two, but similarly described by the annotation vectors containing only 1's and 2's.

Given the description of Figures 2b and 2c above, it should be clear what is happening in the more complex Figures 2d and 2e. In these, the upper bound is similarly described by the polarised case between the first and last labels, whereas the lower bounds are described by the polarised cases between successive labels. This gives rise to the effect that subjectivity minima appear at each ordinal label (i.e., when all annotators selected that label) and that a single maxima appears at complexity = 0.5, when half the annotators selected the lowest possible annotation and the other half selected the highest.

Considering Figure 2e, which represents the original labels in the LCP2021 data, we see that the spread of annotations covers almost the entire possible space. We can observe that lower subjectivity occurs at the two ends of the scale (0.0 and 4.0), with similarly lower values for subjectivity appearing at 1.0 and 3.0. Interestingly, where there should be a minima at 2.0, this is missing, indicating that annotators were unlikely to agree on the 'Neutral' category in the annotation scheme. The observed maxima is around 1.75, indicating that the top portion of potential subjectivity values is missing as the maximum possible subjectivity would be 2.0.

We also analysed the threshold for subjectivity prediction and report our results in Figure 2f. This follows an inverse-S curve, in line with the normal distribution of subjectivity shown in Figure 2a. Again, we are not seeking to give a specific value for the subjectivity threshold here, but rather attempting to expose the behaviour of the thresholded values. We can see that a threshold of 0.25 ($\alpha = 0.005$) will result in around 95% of terms being considered subjective, whereas a threshold of 0.5 ($\alpha = 0.01$) will result in around 60% of the terms being considered subjective.

5. CWI2018 vs. LCP2021

Using the data above we can draw several comparisons between the two prominent existing datasets for CWI/LCP annotation. First of all it is clear from Figures 1a and 2a that the underlying distribution of subjectivity in CWI2018 and LCP2021 is fundamentally different. This is due to the existence of many more agreed upon simple terms in CWI2018. By comparison, the LCP2021 data contains much more subjectivity than the CWI2018 data. Whereas the majority of instances in the latter dataset have a subjectivity close to 0, the subjectivity in the LCP data is centered around 0.4-0.6 (i.e., around half a point on the Likert scale). This is a factor of the way in which each dataset was annotated. In the CWI2018 data, annotators were presented with a context and asked to identify any complex terms. If a term was identified by at least one annotator, it was included in the dataset. This leads to the case where many terms were annotated by only a single annotator, having an annotation vector with a single 1 and the rest 0's. In our definition of complexity/subjectivity this is labelled as low-complexity, low-subjectivity. But it may be the case that the non-annotations of the term are really just the other annotators neglecting to annotate that term, rather than a confirmation of the term's simplicity. Contrastingly, the LCP2021 data presented annotators with specific terms and requested an annotation decision for every given term. This means that every annotation in the dataset is representative of a meaningful decision by the annotator. Clearly, this has led to more subjectivity in the range of annotations that are returned for LCP2021 than CWI2018.

The range of subjectivity with respect to complexity values is also larger in the LCP2021 data as a result of the labels on a 5-point Likert scale that were employed. This can be seen when comparing Figure 1b to Figure 2e. Whereas for the CWI2018 data, the subjectivity values are linked directly to the complexity, the LCP2021 data has a range of subjectivity values for each complexity value. This is because each possible complexity value could be made up of many different annotation vectors. E.g., a complexity value of 2 could be made up of 10 annotations of 2 or 5 annotation of 1 and 5 annotations of 3, as well as many other ways. Whereas the former would have a low subjectivity value, the latter would have a higher subjectivity as the annotators agreed less.

The subjectivity threshold behaves in a similar way between the two datasets. Both produce an inverse S-curve in Figures 1c and 2f. The α value was used to determine common thresholds and across our 2 datasets it allows for a similar threshold to be set given different values of α. Further work on datasets with different values of n and L is needed to determine the robustness of α to these values. Both curves follow a stepped curve, due to the different values that could be produced by the formula for subjectivity operating on a fixed size vector of integers. The LCP2021 data has more levels, producing a smoother curve as it has more labels in the annotation scheme — allowing for a wider range of final values.

We further compared the subjectivity values for common words between the CWI2018 and LCP2021 datasets. To do this, we took the subset of instances containing tokens that occurred in both datasets ($n = 26166$) and calculated Pearson's correlation between the subjectivity values in both datasets. The correlation was low at 0.189, indicating that the subjectivity for specific words in the two datasets is not well-aligned. This may seem surprising, as we would expect subjective words in one dataset to also be subjective in another dataset, however given the findings presented so far on the nature of subjectivity in each dataset and the description of the differing annotation protocols employed, it is conceivable that the discrepancy is in fact due to the differences in the datasets' construction and that future datasets following either protocol would have higher correlation.

6. Factors Affecting Subjectivity

To investigate our second research question, we adopt the LCP2021 data and perform a correlation analysis with a number of features which are used elsewhere in the literature to determine the complexity of a word. The feature categories and specific features, with identifiers are listed below:

Lexical Ambiguity:

Number of WordNet Senses (LA1): The number of synsets that the wordform appears in within WordNet.

WordNet Tree Depth (LA2): The depth at which this word appears in the WordNet Tree.

Number of WordNet Hyponyms (LA3): The number of hyponyms (words with a more specific meaning) that this word has in WordNet.

Lexical Frequency:

Web1T Frequency (LF1): The frequency of the term in the Google Web1T unigram dataset (Brants and Franz, 2006).

Subtlex Frequency (LF2): The frequency of the term in the Subtlex dataset (Van Heuven et al., 2014).

log Web1T Frequency (LF3): $log(\text{LF1})$

log Subtlex Frequency (LF4): $log(\text{LF2})$

MRC Psycholinguistic Norms:

Familiarity (PN1): How likely the word is to be known.

Concreteness (PN2): The degree to which the word represents a grounded concept.

Imageability (PN3): The degree to which the referent of a term can be visualised.

We use Pearson's correlation to determine the relationship between the subjectivity values for LCP2021 and the features we have determined above. These are presented in Table 3, where we also include the correlation with complexity for reference. The correlation between the complexity and subjectivity values was 0.641.

Table 3 shows that the features we tried have a weak negative correlation with subjectivity. The correlation with the lowest magnitude (LA2, WordNet Tree Depth) is -0.094 and the highest (LF4, Log SUBTLEX Frequency) is -0.412. The correlation values for subjectivity are typically in line with, although slightly lower than those for complexity, except in the case of LA2 and LF3, which both show a larger discrepancy, although the reason for this is unclear.

7. Predicting Subjectivity

Finally, we train several models to predict subjectivity in the LCP2021 dataset. This could enable future applications to not only determine which words are complex or simple, but also determine whether a word is likely to split the opinions of users. This may be useful for determining simplification and personalisation strategies, or for better understanding the nature of a complexity value that is returned by a system. For example, if a system returns a neutral complexity, it is helpful to know if that value is likely to be agreed upon, or if some users will find the word difficult, whereas others will find it easy (giving an average of neutral).

We first select a subjectivity threshold of 0.68, which splits the data into 50% subjective and 50% non-subjective. Duplicate tokens in the dataset were removed, leaving 5,617 instances. We did not take contexts into account, as our features are context-free. We then created a training (70%) and testing (30%) set for our experiments.

We selected a Support Vector Machine (SVM), Random Forest (RF) and AdaBoost (AB) classifier from SciKitLearn and trained each one on our dataset. We did not tune the hyperparameters. We used all features described previously in Section 6. All results are reported on a single final run on the test set. We report the Precision, Recall and F1 score for both the Subjective and Non-Subjective classes in Table 4.

Our results are intended to demonstrate that subjectivity can be predicted using the features we have identified, as well as to give some simple baseline results for performance on this task. The scores indicate a reasonable predictive power, with AdaBoost giving an F1 score of 0.713 on the subjective class and 0.645 on the non-subjective class.

8. Discussion

8.1. Answers to Research Hypotheses

The answers to our initial research hypotheses stated earlier are given below:

RH1.1: We demonstrated that we could identify subjective and non-subjective annotations through the use of an equation for determining a subjectivity value and setting a threshold. We investigated the nature of subjectivity in the CWI2018 and LCP2021 datasets and demonstrated that both datasets contain a range of subjective and non-subjective annotations.

RH1.2: We found a low correlation between the subjectivity values for common terms in the two datasets we studied. Our analysis showed that the nature of subjectivity in these datasets is different, leading to the discrepancy.

RH2.1–2.3: We demonstrated that all of our feature categories had a low, but meaningful correlation with subjectivity. The features that we selected are also correlative with complexity and, as subjectivity and complexity are correlative with each other, we were able to use these features for subjectivity too.

	LA1	LA2	LA3	LF1	LF2	LF3	LF4	PN1	PN2	PN3
Complexity	-0.387	-0.229	-0.197	-0.330	-0.246	-0.443	-0.573	-0.351	-0.331	-0.314
Subjectivity	-0.265	-0.094	-0.167	-0.283	-0.222	-0.271	-0.412	-0.274	-0.258	-0.245

Table 3: Correlation analysis between common lexical features and complexity/subjectivity in the LCP2021 dataset

Method	Subjective			Non-Subjective		
	P	R	F1	P	R	F1
RF	0.658	0.681	0.669	0.656	**0.632**	0.644
SVM	0.623	**0.836**	**0.714**	**0.736**	0.476	0.579
AB	**0.660**	0.775	0.713	0.715	0.586	**0.645**

Table 4: Results of predicting which instances in the dataset will be subjective

RH3.1: We were able to predict the subjective label of the words in the LCP2021 dataset with an F1 score of 0.71. This demonstrates that subjectivity is a predictable phenomenon and we hope that in light of this finding future researchers will consider complexity in light of subjectivity.

8.2. Threats to Validity

One deficiency in our work is that we have not taken context into account. In the LCP2021 and CWI2018 annotations words were presented in context and the labels were given for the word in context, not for the word itself. This meant that repeated instances of a word had different annotation vectors and hence complexity labels (as different word senses, etc. affected the complexity). In our work, we have selected a single instance of each token, reducing the dataset size and ignoring the context. We expect to be able to address this in future work by investigating the context sensitivity of lexical subjectivity, in relation to complexity as well as other tasks.

The definition of complexity was formalised for this paper. Whilst this is reflective of the processes undertaken in previous papers to the best of the authors knowledge and given the reporting in previous work, it is possible that some unreported factors of the process are missing from our definitions. The measure of subjectivity was also determined within the scope of this work and is not adopted widely by the community. We hope that this work will introduce the notion of subjectivity and allow researchers working on lexical complexity to consider their annotations in the context of subjectivity.

Finally, a threat to the validity is that the work is done on secondary datasets. In the scope of this work, we have no control over the quality of the annotations that have been undertaken. Each dataset is reported on extensively in its own paper which detail the quality control mechanisms used to ensure that the annotators were doing the task expected of them.

9. Related Work

Complex Word Identification was first proposed as an initial step in the lexical simplification pipeline (Devlin, 1998). Efforts to automatically predict complex words (Shardlow, 2013) using machine learning techniques showed this to be possible. The task was popularised by shared tasks (Paetzold and Specia, 2016; Yimam et al., 2018), where winning systems typically used feature based approaches (Gooding and Kochmar, 2018). Recently, the LCP2021 shared task (Shardlow et al., 2021) introduced continuous complexity prediction, as opposed to the binary or probabilistic prediction seen prior. High-ranking systems used either transformer based models (Yaseen et al., 2021) or feature engineering approaches (Mosquera, 2021).

Further work in CWI/LCP has sought to adapt the problem to a personalising task (Lee and Yeung, 2018) in which the specific needs of a user are modelled and reflected in individualised complexity predictions. Recent work demonstrated that lexical complexity differs due to annotator background, such as native speakers vs. non-native speakers (Gooding et al., 2021).

The distribution of lexical complexity shown in this work is backed up by previous works from the literature analysing the CWI-2018 dataset (Quijada and Medero, 2016). This data, and by association the concept of lexical complexity, has been considered subjective previously by other authors (Finnimore et al., 2019).

In the field of sentiment analysis the term subjectivity is used to refer to the degree to which a user is drawing on their own personal opinion vs. stating objective fact (Maks and Vossen, 2012; Hill and Korhonen, 2014). That is a subtly different notion of subjectivity to the one used here. In the context of Lexical Complexity Prediction, we are assuming that a user's annotations are inherently drawn from personal experience, and instead our measure is whether those personal experiences converge or diverge.

10. Conclusion

We have investigated the nature of Lexical subjectivity within the scope of lexical complexity. We show that this exists across two prominent datasets and outline how it differs between them. We have also shown that subjectivity is not a stochastic phenomenon, but is correlated to several well-known features for lexical complexity and that we are able to predict subjectivity with simple machine learning classifiers in an unseen setting. We expect that transformer based methodologies will also provide strong scores on this task, and leave these experiments to future work. We release the datasets with subjectivity values, and the code used to create them via GitHub[2].

11. Bibliographical References

Devlin, S. (1998). The use of a psycholinguistic database in the simplification of text for aphasic readers. *Linguistic databases*.

Ehara, Y. (2020). Interpreting neural CWI classifiers' weights as vocabulary size. In *Proceedings of the Fifteenth Workshop on Innovative Use of NLP for Building Educational Applications*, pages 171–176, Seattle, WA, USA → Online, July. Association for Computational Linguistics.

Finnimore, P., Fritzsch, E., King, D., Sneyd, A., Ur Rehman, A., Alva-Manchego, F., and Vlachos, A. (2019). Strong baselines for complex word identification across multiple languages. In *Proceedings of the 2019 Conference of the North American Chapter of the Association for Computational Linguistics: Human Language Technologies, Volume 1 (Long and Short Papers)*, pages 970–977, Minneapolis, Minnesota, June. Association for Computational Linguistics.

Gooding, S. and Kochmar, E. (2018). Camb at cwi shared task 2018: Complex word identification with ensemble-based voting. In *Proceedings of the Thirteenth Workshop on Innovative Use of NLP for Building Educational Applications*, pages 184–194.

Gooding, S., Kochmar, E., Yimam, S. M., and Biemann, C. (2021). Word complexity is in the eye of the beholder. In *Proceedings of the 2021 Conference of the North American Chapter of the Association for Computational Linguistics: Human Language Technologies*, pages 4439–4449.

Hill, F. and Korhonen, A. (2014). Concreteness and subjectivity as dimensions of lexical meaning. In *Proceedings of the 52nd Annual Meeting of the Association for Computational Linguistics (Volume 2: Short Papers)*, pages 725–731, Baltimore, Maryland, June. Association for Computational Linguistics.

Lee, J. S. and Yeung, C. Y. (2018). Personalizing lexical simplification. In *Proceedings of the 27th International Conference on Computational Linguistics*, pages 224–232.

Maks, I. and Vossen, P. (2012). A lexicon model for deep sentiment analysis and opinion mining applications. *Decision Support Systems*, 53(4):680–688.

Mosquera, A. (2021). Alejandro mosquera at semeval-2021 task 1: Exploring sentence and word features for lexical complexity prediction. In *Proceedings of the 15th International Workshop on Semantic Evaluation (SemEval-2021)*, pages 554–559.

[2]https://github.com/MMU-TDMLab/LCP_Subjectivity

Paetzold, G. and Specia, L. (2016). Semeval 2016 task 11: Complex word identification. In *Proceedings of the 10th International Workshop on Semantic Evaluation (SemEval-2016)*, pages 560–569.

Quijada, M. and Medero, J. (2016). HMC at SemEval-2016 task 11: Identifying complex words using depth-limited decision trees. In *Proceedings of the 10th International Workshop on Semantic Evaluation (SemEval-2016)*, pages 1034–1037, San Diego, California, June. Association for Computational Linguistics.

Shardlow, M., Evans, R., Paetzold, G., and Zampieri, M. (2021). Semeval-2021 task 1: Lexical complexity prediction. In *Proceedings of the 15th International Workshop on Semantic Evaluation (SemEval-2021)*, pages 1–16.

Shardlow, M. (2013). A comparison of techniques to automatically identify complex words. In *51st Annual Meeting of the Association for Computational Linguistics Proceedings of the Student Research Workshop*, pages 103–109.

Yaseen, T. B., Ismail, Q., Al-Omari, S., Al-Sobh, E., and Abdullah, M. (2021). Just-blue at semeval-2021 task 1: Predicting lexical complexity using bert and roberta pre-trained language models. In *Proceedings of the 15th International Workshop on Semantic Evaluation (SemEval-2021)*, pages 661–666.

Yimam, S. M., Biemann, C., Malmasi, S., Paetzold, G., Specia, L., Štajner, S., Tack, A., and Zampieri, M. (2018). A report on the complex word identification shared task 2018. In *Proceedings of the Thirteenth Workshop on Innovative Use of NLP for Building Educational Applications*, pages 66–78.

Zampieri, M., Malmasi, S., Paetzold, G., and Specia, L. (2017). Complex word identification: Challenges in data annotation and system performance. *NLPTEA 2017*, page 59.

12. Language Resource References

Brants, T. and Franz, A. (2006). Web 1t 5-gram version 1 (2006). *Linguistic Data Consortium, Philadelphia*.

Shardlow, M., Evans, R., and Zampieri, M. (2022). Predicting lexical complexity in english texts: the complex 2.0 dataset. *Language Resources and Evaluation*, pages 1–42.

Van Heuven, W. J., Mandera, P., Keuleers, E., and Brysbaert, M. (2014). Subtlex-uk: A new and improved word frequency database for british english. *Quarterly journal of experimental psychology*, 67(6):1176–1190.

Yimam, S. M., Štajner, S., Riedl, M., and Biemann, C. (2017). Cwig3g2-complex word identification task across three text genres and two user groups. In *Proceedings of the Eighth International Joint Conference on Natural Language Processing (Volume 2: Short Papers)*, pages 401–407.

Proceedings of the 2nd READI Workshop @ LREC2022, pages 17–24
Marseille, 24 June 2022

A Dictionary-Based Study of Word Sense Difficulty

David Alfter, Rémi Cardon and Thomas François
CENTAL
Université catholique de Louvain, Belgium
{first.last}@uclouvain.be

Abstract

In this article, we present an exploratory study on perceived word sense difficulty by native and non-native speakers of French. We use a graded lexicon in conjunction with the French Wiktionary to generate tasks in bundles of four items. Annotators manually rate the difficulty of the word senses based on their usage in a sentence by selecting the easiest and the most difficult word sense out of four. Our results show that the native and non-native speakers largely agree when it comes to the difficulty of words. Further, the rankings derived from the manual annotation broadly follow the levels of the words in the graded resource, although these levels were not overtly available to annotators. Using clustering, we investigate whether there is a link between the complexity of a definition and the difficulty of the associated word sense. However, results were inconclusive. The annotated data set will be made available for research purposes.

Keywords: word difficulty, readability, lexicography

1. Introduction

Dictionaries are used by native speakers of a language and by language learners when they want to learn or check the meaning of a word. Even though there are dictionaries that are specifically targeted at learners, other widely known online dictionaries such as Wiktionary[1] may be one of the first resources that comes to mind. Along with definitions, those resources provide the users with examples of use for words.

In this article, we want to check how useful these examples are in helping users with understanding words. The hypothesis for this research question is that non-native speakers can assess the difficulty of the meaning of a word when they see it used in a sentence, in the same way readers can infer the meaning of words based on the context (Miller et al., 1996; Miller, 1999). We observe how word difficulty is rated both by native and non-native speakers. We also assess whether a single word sense is rated differently based on the example of usage.

We also want to check whether dictionary definitions are more difficult when the word meanings themselves are more difficult. On the terminological side, it should be noted that *complexity* can be seen as an inherent property of a word or text, invariant and independent of the context (Pallotti, 2015), whereas *difficulty* can be seen as a construct that arises when a given reader interacts with a given word or text; *difficulty* varies from reader to reader. However, the distinction between these two categories is not always very clear, even in the literature on the topic.

In an effort to clarify the terminological question, we detail the operationalizations of the concepts used in this paper: (1) in the data annotation, we look at lexical *difficulty* to choose words, since our selection is based on proficiency levels from a learner-targeted vocabulary resource; (2) we also assess words in terms of lexical *difficulty*, since the ratings we collect are based on the annotators' intuition; (3) in the second experiment, the *complexity* of definitions is approximated through the lens of readability research, i.e. by characterizing the definitions using a number of linguistic variables. The hypothesis here is that it is more difficult to explain difficult words, thus leading to a potentially more verbose explanation (that might nonetheless still be easy to understand); this is parallel to the idea that "languages encode conceptually more complex meanings with longer linguistic forms" (Lewis and Frank, 2016).

In order to assess these hypotheses, we performed various experiments with resources in French.

For the first hypothesis, we asked native speakers of French and non-native speakers of French to rate word difficulty based on their use in dictionary examples. To do so, seven annotators rated word difficulty by only having access to dictionary examples. The annotated data will be made available for research purposes. We surmise that the data might be useful for the evaluation of complex word identification systems. One contribution of this part of the work is that the resource is annotated at the sense level, and not at the word level, which – to the best of our knowledge – is something that has not been done before for French.

For the second hypothesis, we explore the correlation between the ranking of the words difficulty produced by the annotators and the readability of the definitions.

In section 3, we describe the data that we used as a source for our linguistic material. Section 4 describes the experimental protocol that we put in place. Results are presented in section 5 and discussed in section 6.

2. Related Work

Word lists are often used in second language learning scenarios (e.g. Laufer and Nation (1999; O'Dell

[1] en.wiktionary.org/

et al. (2000; Meara (2002; Gu (2003; Nation (2013)). However, word lists compiled from L1 material are rarely suitable for L2 purposes (Richards (1974, p.72); François et al. (2014, p.3767)). There are some resources such as the CEFRLex family[2] that are based on L2 textbooks, thus directly targeting second language learners. However, even such resources generally use lemmas as primary entries, conflating different word senses. Especially from a language learning perspective, it is to be argued that not all word senses are learned at once, and thus basing vocabulary knowledge on lists where word senses are conflated is potentially misleading. Further, more frequent words (that are generally taught early, since frequency is often taken as a proxy for complexity, e.g. Rayner and Duffy (1986)) also tend to have more senses than less frequently used words (Crossley et al., 2010).

For English, there exists a dataset that is annotated both for lexical complexity and word senses, SeCoDa (Strohmaier et al., 2020), leveraging the Cambridge Advanced Learner's Dictionary[3].

However, even the shared tasks organized on the topic of Complex Word Identification (CWI; cf. (Paetzold and Specia, 2016; Yimam et al., 2018)) and Lexical Complexity Prediction (LCP; cf. (Shardlow et al., 2021)) do not explicitly distinguish between the complexity of different word senses; while some data sets do indeed present words in context, thus disambiguation of the words. That said, this information is not directly operationalized.

To the best of our knowledge, there is no work on using dictionaries to disambiguate vocabulary lists for French. Regarding the investigation of the complexity of definitions with regards to the complexity of their head words, we did not find any systematic study. We only found one article working on the complexity of dictionary definitions (Gross, 2018). However, the author states that a true semantic definition of a word (especially nouns) should not be conceptual but contain the whole set of appropriate predicates for this noun. This is not directly in line with our approach, as we work with conceptual definitions.

3. Data

3.1. Source

The data for our experiment comes from two different resources.

As we want to relate the outcome of the experiment to second language learning, we base ourselves on the French textbook-derived vocabulary list FLELex (François et al., 2014). FLELex lists words as well as their frequencies observed across different proficiency levels. In order to divide FLELex into six discrete levels, we use the machine learning based level assignment proposed by Pintard and François (2020) which is freely available through the CEFRLex webpage[4]. It contains 14,236 rated words.

As we work at the word sense level, we rely on a dictionary resource. The resource we use is GLAWI (Sajous and Hathout, 2015). GLAWI is an XML version of the French Wiktionary[5]. GLAWI's senses are strongly fine-grained : in the list we extracted, the average number of definitions per lemma is 13. We also calculated the median value, which is 2.

We filter GLAWI to extract the words that are found in FLELex. Every lemma, sense, definition or example that we mention throughout the article is extracted from the resulting subset.

3.2. Anchor Words

In order to "anchor" the relative difficulty rankings obtained with the methodology (cf. Section 4), we included "anchors", i.e. words that have a reliable fixed difficulty level. Anchor words were chosen among monosemous words that show a strong centrality for their respective level, i.e. words that are likely to be representative of a given level, based on the continuous numerical score N_c introduced in Gala et al. (2013):

$$N_c = N_i + e^{-r}, r = \frac{\Sigma_{k=1}^{i} U_k}{\Sigma_{k=i+1}^{N} U_k} \quad (1)$$

N_c is calculated for a given level N_i which corresponds to the level of first occurrence, i.e. the first level at which a word is observed with a frequency greater than 0, and modifies the level score by a score $e^{-r} \in [0, 1[$. r is calculated as the ratio of frequencies U_k, with U_k the frequency at level $k \in [1, N]$. In other words, r indicates the cumulative frequency up to level i divided by the remaining cumulative frequencies after level i. High values of e^{-r} indicate that there exists a non-negligible frequency mass outside of level N_i, while low values of e^{-r} indicate that the main frequency mass is located at level N_i.

For the selection of anchor words, we calculated N_c for all words in FLELex, excluded all words that did not fullfil the criterion $e^{-r} < 0.1$, and manually selected 5 words per level for a total of 30 anchor words.[6]

4. Experiments

4.1. Data Combination

For this experiment, we use a similar setup as in (Alfter et al., 2021), i.e. we arrange the example sentences into sets of four and ask annotators to select the easiest

[2]https://cental.uclouvain.be/cefrlex

[3]https://dictionary.cambridge.org/dictionary/english/

[4]https://cental.uclouvain.be/cefrlex/flelex/

[5]https://fr.wiktionary.org/

[6]While this methodology of level assignment differs from the methodology by (Pintard and François, 2020), it allows for a more fine-grained assessment of "centrality", and given that we work on a restricted subset of items where $e^{-r} < 0.1$, the items under scrutiny are of comparable quality with regards to automatic level assignment.

and the hardest of the words, a technique called best-word scaling (Louviere et al., 2015). A set of four items constitutes one *task* (see figure 1).
We use the combinatorial redundancy reducing algorithm (Alfter et al., 2021) for calculating the optimal number of tasks with minimal redundancy. This number, for 120 examples, comes to 1300. Each example is shown between 40 and 49 times in different combinations with other examples.
Care was taken to arrange the examples in such a manner that the four examples illustrating the same word but different senses end up as one task each.

4.2. Data Selection

For the experiment, we work at the definition (i.e. sense) level of words. We use example sentences from definitions as illustrations of a certain word sense.
In order to explore the different hypotheses, data was automatically selected according to the following criteria:

- 5 anchor words per level ($5 * 6 = 30$)
- 4 examples (= 1 task) per level that illustrate the same word but different senses ($4 * 6 = 24$)
- 4 examples (= 1 task) per level that illustrate the same word and same sense but with different examples ($4 * 6 = 24$)
- 3 paired examples per level, i.e. two examples of the same word but with different senses, chosen among words with at least two senses ($3 * 2 * 6 = 36$)
- 6 randomly chosen examples that have at least two senses

Thus, the total number of examples in the experiment is $30 + 24 + 24 + 36 + 6 = 120$. While this may seem like a relatively small number of items, we surmise that it is a sufficient amount for an exploratory work with an acceptable trade-off between quantity of items and annotation time.

4.3. Annotation

For the experimental design, we use a custom graphical user interface shown in Figure 1.[7] The user interface presents four sentences with one or more word(s) marked in bold and in purple, which is the word to be judged. After each sentence, we also display the lemma of the word. On the left side and right side of the examples are buttons to choose the easiest and hardest expressions. After selecting a word as being the easiest or hardest, the color of the lemma respectively changes to green and red in order to also reflect the choice visually.

[7]The interface shows a translated mockup. Note that the English Wiktionary indicates *years* (plural) as a lemma for the second example: `https://en.wiktionary.org/wiki/years`.

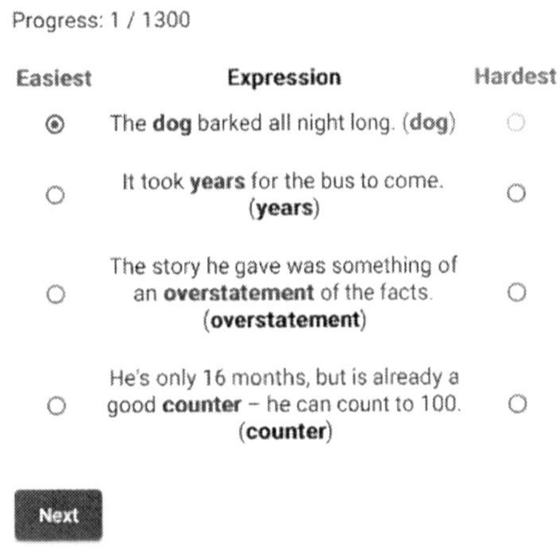

Figure 1: Graphical user interface with 'dog' being selected as easiest sense.

The user interface is designed to be simple and intuitive to use. It is possible to stop annotation at any time and resume later at the point where one left off. Further, the interface can be accessed from different devices such as laptops, computers, or smartphones, and one can freely switch between devices. The interface automatically registers the time elapsed between the completion of two tasks.
The user interface also attempts to enforce valid answers by disallowing clicking next if no choice has been made or if only one side contains a choice.
Internally, the example chosen as easiest is assigned a score of 1, the example chosen as hardest a score of 3 and the two examples not selected a score of 2. In the end, all votes v_{ij} for item i are aggregated into a single score s_i, with $i \in [1, 120]$ and $j \in [1, n]$, n being the number of votes for item i:

$$s_i = \frac{\Sigma_{j=1}^{n} v_{ij}}{n} \quad (2)$$

In order to see whether annotators are consistent in their annotation, we duplicated one task as control task. After shuffling of the data, the control task was inserted at positions 4 and 1299 (of 1300).
For this experiment, we recruited two student helpers who were paid 12€ per hour as well as three colleagues. In total, including two of the authors, seven people contributed to the experiment.
Each time they access the interface (unless requested otherwise, using an opt-out option in the form of a checkbox), users see a page displaying the instructions. Here is a translation (from French) of the detailed instructions displayed for the task (we leave out the instructions related to the interface):

> You will see sets with 4 sentences followed by the lemma of the word in bold. We ask you, for each set, to indicate which of the emphasized word's meanings seems to be

> the most difficult to understand for you, and which one seems to be the easiest.
>
> Don't think for too long, use your intuition.
>
> Judge only the item in bold, with reference to its dictionary form (e.g., verbs in the subjunctive mood should be judged as equal to verbs in the indicative mood).
>
> Context is given to indicate the sense of the word and should not have an influence on the judgment.

The annotators were orally asked to avoid discussing the tasks between themselves before completion.
Table 1 gives an overview over the demographic information of the participants.

Gender	
Male	4
Female	3
Mother tongue	
French	4
Japanese	1
Spanish	1
Luxembourgish	1

Table 1: Demographic information of participants

Each annotator was asked to complete all 1300 tasks.

4.4. Definition Complexity Evaluation

To assess definition complexity, we randomly selected 30,000 definitions from words that appear in FLELex. We processed them through FABRA, the French Aggregator-Based Readability Assessment Toolkit (Wilkens et al., 2022) and performed clustering on the data. FABRA calculates in excess of 4,000 features for each sentence. We restricted FABRA features to surface (e.g. word length) and lexical (e.g. frequency in different word lists) features, as the other classes of features (syntactic and discourse features) are more suitable to full text, and definition texts are not necessarily complete sentences. Before clustering, we perform dimensionality reduction (to 100 dimension) using Principal Component Analysis (PCA) (Pearson, 1901) as implemented in scikit-learn (Pedregosa et al., 2011). For clustering, we use the KMeans (Lloyd, 1957; MacQueen, 1967) implementation also available in scikit-learn, with the number of clusters set to 6 in order to match the number of CEFR levels, which are used by the FLELEX resource.

We then look at the cluster to which every definition linked to word senses that were annotated correspond, to check whether we can observe a correlation between the clusters and the difficulty level.

5. Results

5.1. Time per Annotator

Using a preliminary (randomly chosen) set of items, the authors tested the platform in order to estimate the time investment necessary. We found that it took about 12 seconds to complete one task. Based on this estimation and adding some margin (20 seconds per task), we estimated the total time needed to complete the experiment at around 7 hours.
Table 2 shows the average time taken for a single task, per annotator, in seconds. As the interface counts the number of seconds between the completion of two tasks, as long as annotators leave the interface open before continuing, time is being counted. By excluding outlier values – outliers being values of more than 90 seconds (an arbitrarily chosen threshold corresponding to an implausible time for a single task completion) – we obtain the average time per task as shown on the right side in Table 2 (Avg time excl. outl.), which is much closer to the originally predicted time per task.

Annotator	Avg time (s)	Avg time excl. outl.
1	15	12
2	101	9
3	12	9
4	45	18
5	39	16
6	78	8
7	11	11

Table 2: Average time per task per annotator

5.2. Rankings

In order to compute a ranking, we calculate the score of each item according to equation 2 in three different ways: taking into account all annotators, only native speakers, and only non-native speakers. This gives us three rankings: the global ranking, the native ranking, and the non-native ranking. Due to space limitations, the full results are not included here but can be retrieved at `https://github.com/daalft/dicomplex`.
Overall, the three rankings are very similar, the most dissimilar being the ranking between native and non-native speakers. However, even the most dissimilar rankings are highly correlated (Pearson's rank correlation coefficient of 0.90) as detailed in Section 5.3. A qualitative analysis reveals that there are mainly differences in rank for the words *haltérophilie* 'weight lifting', on rank 73 in the native speaker ranking and rank 115 in the non-native speaker ranking (a difference of 42 ranks), and *chèvrefeuille* 'honeysuckle', rank 78 vs 101 (difference of 23 ranks). These words seem to be relatively well known by native speakers, but introduced very late for non-native speakers. Two other notable differences can be found between *bricoleur* 'tin-

kerer', rank 28 in the native ranking versus rank 43 in the non-native ranking, and *clignotant* 'indicator/turn signal', rank 33 versus rank 49.

As regards the influence of context on the perceived difficulty of a word sense, we can see that the different examples of the same word sense end up rather close together on the ranking, with a maximum span (i.e. the difference between the maximum and minimum rank) of 19 ranks and an average span of about 14, as illustrated in Table 3. Furthermore, one can see that the words follow the progression of CEFR levels, except for *guérison* 'recovery' which ends up closer to B1 level yet shows a very narrow clustering.

Word	Level	Ranks	Span
connaître 'to know'	A1	13, 17, 23, 27	14
fixer 'to fix'	A2	31, 39, 40, 46	15
joindre 'to join'	B1	48, 52, 56, 67	19
prétention 'pretention'	B2	92, 96, 100, 105	13
guérison 'recovery'	C1	47, 49, 50, 54	7
attirail 'paraphernalia'	C2	95, 99, 107, 110	15

Table 3: Ranks of examples of the same word sense

The biggest rank span is found for *joindre* 'to join'. Upon closer inspection, we can see that the example sentence at rank 67 is *Ces planches, cette porte, ces fenêtres ne* ***joignent*** *pas bien.* 'These planks, this door, these windows do not **join** well', which is indeed a rather rare use of *joindre*.

We can see that the different senses of a word end up at quite different ranks, as illustrated in Table 4. The maximum observed span is 66 for 'point', with an average span of about 34, a significantly higher span than for examples of the same sense. An exception to the wider spread is the word 'old'. Upon closer inspection, we can see that the example sentences that were automatically selected were very short and thus did not convey the fine-grained meaning distinctions ('old' as pertaining to a certain age of a person, ancient, a derogatory term, a term of veneration). On the other hand, *point* 'point/dot/stitch pattern' ranged from *point* 'dot' (e.g., a *dot* ends a sentence) to *point* 'stitch pattern', and the meaning of stitch pattern was ranked as hardest of the senses by a large margin (rank 74, the closest rank of other meanings being rank 28). Again, one can also see that the ranking order follows the CEFR levels from FLELex in broad terms.

Table 5 shows the rank positions of all anchor words for the global ranking, the native speaker ranking and the

Word	Level	Ranks	Span
vieux 'old'	A1	3, 4, 5, 6	3
point 'point/dot/stitch pattern'	A2	8, 25, 28, 74	66
repasser 'to iron/pass again/redo'	B1	30, 58, 65, 79	49
perte 'loss/ruin'	B2	32, 33, 53, 61	29
pétiller 'to fizz/sparkle/crackle'	C1	73, 101, 104, 111	38
fausser 'to falsify/forge/fake'	C2	76, 83, 85, 97	21

Table 4: Ranks of examples of different word senses

non-native speaker ranking. As can be observed, there is a clear progression from A1 to C2, with expected overlaps between adjacent levels. Further, the rankings are quite similar, although the non-native ranking seems to follow FLELex levels a bit more closely, which is to be expected, since FLELex is a second language learner oriented resource.

5.3. Intra- and Inter-Annotator Agreement

Based on the control task that was annotated twice by each annotator, we can see that five out of seven annotators were completely consistent in their annotation. For the remaining two annotators, one person chose a different "easiest" word while the other person chose a different "most difficult" word. As the control task was randomly chosen, there was no expectation regarding which word should be considered the easiest or the most difficult. Furthermore, the two annotators in question still remained consistent in their other choice, hence we neither discard the these annotators nor proceed in any kind of remediation.

Inter-annotator agreement (Pearson's rank correlation coefficient) shows a high agreement of 0.90 between the ranking of native speakers and the ranking of non-native speakers. This seems to confirm that non-native speakers can produce native-like rankings. This is consistent with what has been found in a similar study (cf. Alfter et al. (2021)).

5.4. Clustering

Figure 2a shows a visualization of the clustering using t-distributed stochastic neighbor embedding (t-SNE; (Van der Maaten and Hinton, 2008), a popular tech-

Global ranking		Native ranking		Non-native ranking	
CEFR level	Word	CEFR level	Word	CEFR level	Word
A1	bonjour	A1	bonjour	A1	bonjour
A1	copine	A1	copine	A1	copine
A2	vite	A2	vite	A1	confiture
A2	frigo	A2	frigo	A2	frigo
A1	confiture	A1	autocar	A2	vite
A1	vendeur	A1	vendeur	A1	vendeur
A1	autocar	B2	grille-pain	B1	apéro
A2	guitariste	A2	guitariste	A1	autocar
B1	apéro	A1	confiture	A2	guitariste
B2	grille-pain	B1	apéro	B2	grille-pain
A2	bricoleur	B2	revolver	B1	corridor
B2	revolver	A2	bricoleur	B1	vouvoyer
B1	festif	A2	clignotant	B1	festif
A2	clignotant	B1	festif	A2	bricoleur
B1	corridor	B1	corridor	A2	clignotant
B1	vouvoyer	B2	enquêter	B2	enquêter
B2	enquêter	B1	vouvoyer	B2	revolver
B1	vacarme	C2	haltérophilie	C1	arrachage
C1	arrachage	C2	chèvrefeuille	C1	discriminatoire
C2	chèvrefeuille	B1	vacarme	B1	vacarme
C1	discriminatoire	C1	surcoût	C2	chèvrefeuille
C1	surcoût	C1	discriminatoire	C1	surcoût
C2	haltérophilie	C1	arrachage	B2	lugubre
B2	perspicacité	B2	perspicacité	B2	perspicacité
B2	lugubre	B2	lugubre	C1	affligeant
C1	affligeant	C1	affligeant	C2	haltérophilie
C2	inexorable	C2	inexorable	C1	achoppement
C2	enhardir	C2	protéiforme	C2	inexorable
C1	achoppement	C2	enhardir	C2	enhardir
C2	protéiforme	C1	achoppement	C2	protéiforme

Table 5: Anchor words: comparison of ranking order positions for global, native and non-native rankings

nique for dimensionality reduction and visualization of high-dimensional data, and Figure 2b shows a visualization of the clustering using Uniform Manifold Approximation and Projection for Dimension Reduction (UMAP; McInnes et al. (2018)). UMAP is a fast and scalable dimensionality reduction algorithm that is said to be "better at preserving some aspects of global structure of the data than most implementations of t-SNE" (McInnes et al., 2018).

The 102 definitions corresponding to the 120 annotated examples are only found in three clusters out of six. Using the cluster numbers from the t-sne visualization, 48 were found in cluster 0 (red), 16 in cluster 2 (green) and 38 in cluster 4 (navy blue). The average scores by cluster, based on the global annotation ranking, are respectively 1.97 (that would be rank 59/120), 2.05 (that would be rank 65/120), and 2.01 (that would be rank 60/120). What we can draw from this observation is that no correlation between the difficulty of a word and the readability of its definition is found in the data we used for our experiments.

6. Discussion and Future Work

While we found the clustering not to correlate with the ranking, we still see a clear delineation of clusters in both visualizations. Further studies should investigate these clusters in more detail to find out what they represent and whether this information might be useful in future studies. From our observations we can get insights about the writing process of a dictionary. For example, the definition of the easy word *pêche* with the meaning of 'peach' is *Fruit du pêcher, parfumé et d'un goût savoureux, dont le très dur noyau est enrobé par une chair jaune ou blanche et une fine peau veloutée de teinte jaune et rouge-orange.* ("Fruit of the peach tree, fragrant and tasty, whose very hard pit is coated by a yellow or white flesh and a thin skin mixed with yellow and red-orange"), while the difficult word *perspicacité* (perceptiveness) is defined with *Pénétration d'esprit* ("Spirit penetration"). Peach is defined in a quite detailed way, while the definition of perceptiveness is abstract and vague. Those are two extreme examples, but it contributes to illustrate why we did not

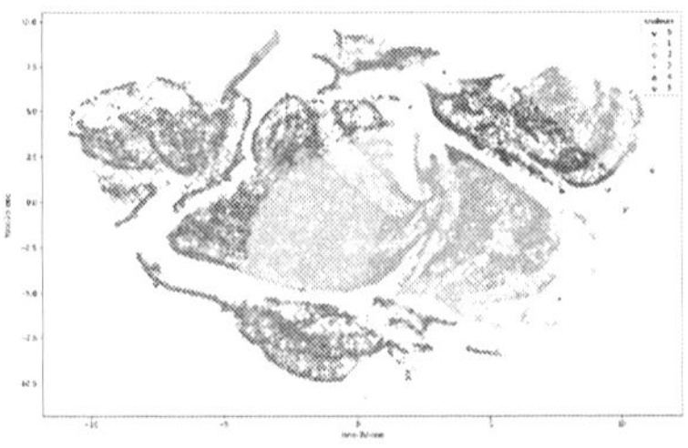

(a) Visualization of clusters using t-SNE

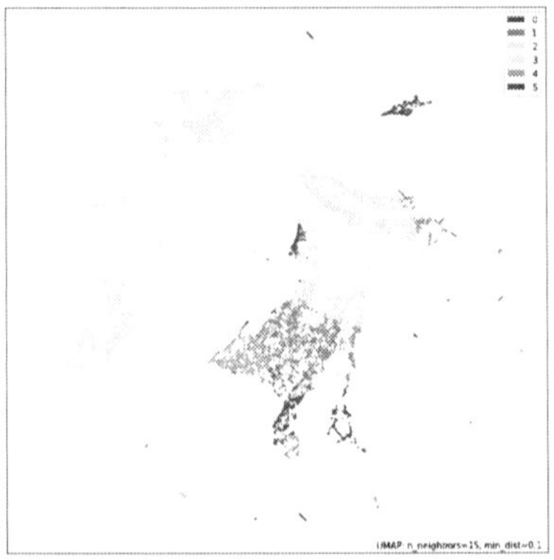

(b) Visualization of clusters using UMAP

find correlations between the readability of definitions and the difficulty of word senses. We believe it would be beneficial to perform more studies on this very aspect, namely with comparing learners' dictionaries and more traditional dictionaries, so as to identify gaps between the phrasing of the definitions and the need of the targeted audience and systematically prevent them.
It would be beneficial to fine-tune the methodology of annotation; the current methodology covers all relations between examples. However, it is possible to drastically reduce the number of comparisons needed by inferring relations based on annotated relations. Thus, for example, – and for simplicity's sake with a simple comparison between two items – if one finds that A is easier than B and that B is easier than C, one could infer that A is easier than C. Thus, one would not need to annotate the relation between A and C. Preliminary experiments have shown that for a binary classification, i.e. choosing the "easiest" of two items, with 100 items, this would require about 700 comparisons between two items. In contrast, using the current methodology and adapting it to the case of binary classification, one would need 4950 comparisons.
It would also be interesting to further explore the differences between annotators, since the question of rater subjectivity has recently become a topic of interest in research on lexical complexity (Gooding et al., 2021; Shardlow, 2022).

7. Conclusion

In this article, we have presented a study on word sense complexity using a graded lexicon with CEFR levels for French and linguistic material (definitions and examples) extracted from the French Wiktionary. We asked seven annotators to rate the complexity of word senses based on their usage in a sentence. The resulting dataset will be made available upon publication. It consists 1,300 sets of four dictionary examples, along with the annotation of which one is the most difficult and which one is the easiest. Those 1,300 sets are found seven times, produced by four French native speakers and three non-native speakers. We have found that native speakers and non-native speakers agree to a quite large extent. However, the clustering was found not to correlate with rankings.
We compared the word senses ranking information to the corresponding definitions in order look for a correlation between a definition's readability and the difficulty of a word. We found no such correlation. Though, by examining closely the data we may argue that assessing the readability of definitions when writing a dictionary could improve its effectiveness.

Acknowledgments

We would like to thank the reviewers for their appreciation of the paper and their numerous detailed comments and suggestions. We also would like to thank our co-raters Nils Bouckaert, Alba Garcia Prades, Angela Kasparian, Hubert Naets and Nami Yamaguchi. David Alfter is supported by the Fonds de la Recherche Scientifique - FNRS under the grant MIS/PGY F.4518.21. Rémi Cardon is supported by the FSR Incoming Postdoc Fellowship program of the FSR - Université Catholique de Louvain.

8. Bibliographical References

Alfter, D., Tiedemann Lindström, T., and Volodina, E. (2021). Crowdsourcing Relative Rankings of Multi-Word Expressions: Experts versus Non-Experts. *Northern European Journal of Language Technology*.

Crossley, S., Salsbury, T., and McNamara, D. (2010). The development of polysemy and frequency use in English second language speakers. *Language Learning*, 60(3):573–605.

François, T., Gala, N., Watrin, P., and Fairon, C. (2014). FLELex: a graded lexical resource for French foreign learners. In *LREC*, pages 3766–3773.

Gala, N., François, T., and Fairon, C. (2013). Towards a French lexicon with difficulty measures: NLP helping to bridge the gap between traditional dictionaries and specialized lexicons. In *eLex-Electronic Lexicography*.

Gooding, S., Kochmar, E., Yimam, S. M., and Biemann, C. (2021). Word complexity is in the eye of the beholder. In *Proceedings of the 2021 Conference of the North American Chapter of the Association for Computational Linguistics: Human Language Technologies*, pages 4439–4449.

Gross, G. (2018). Complexité lexicale: le substantif débat (s). *Neophilologica*, (30):9–24.

Gu, P. Y. (2003). Vocabulary learning in a second language: Person, task, context and strategies. *TESL-EJ*, 7(2):1–25.

Laufer, B. and Nation, P. (1999). A vocabulary-size test of controlled productive ability. *Language testing*, 16(1):33–51.

Lewis, M. L. and Frank, M. C. (2016). The length of words reflects their conceptual complexity. *Cognition*, 153:182–195.

Lloyd, S. (1957). Least square quantization in pcm. bell telephone laboratories paper. published in journal much later: Lloyd, sp: Least squares quantization in pcm. *IEEE Trans. Inform. Theor.(1957/1982)*, 18:11.

Louviere, J. J., Flynn, T. N., and Marley, A. A. J. (2015). *Best-worst scaling: Theory, methods and applications*. Cambridge University Press.

MacQueen, J. (1967). Some methods for classification and analysis of multivariate observations. In *Proceedings of the fifth Berkeley symposium on mathematical statistics and probability*, volume 1, pages 281–297. Oakland, CA, USA.

McInnes, L., Healy, J., and Melville, J. (2018). UMAP: Uniform manifold approximation and projection for dimension reduction. *arXiv preprint arXiv:1802.03426*.

Meara, P. (2002). The rediscovery of vocabulary. *Second Language Research*, 18(4):393–407.

Miller, G. A., Oakhill, J., and Garnham, A. (1996). Contextuality. *Mental models in cognitive science: Essays in honour of Phil Johnson-Laird*, pages 1–18.

Miller, G. A. (1999). On knowing a word. *Annual Review of Psychology*, 50(1):1–19.

Nation, P. (2013). *Learning Vocabulary in Another Language*. Cambridge University Press.

O'Dell, F., Read, J., McCarthy, M., et al. (2000). *Assessing vocabulary*. Cambridge university press.

Paetzold, G. and Specia, L. (2016). SemEval 2016 Task 11: Complex Word Identification. In *SemEval at NAACL-HLT*, pages 560–569.

Pallotti, G. (2015). A simple view of linguistic complexity. *Second Language Research*, 31(1):117–134.

Pearson, K. (1901). On lines and planes of closest fit to systems of points in space. *The London, Edinburgh, and Dublin Philosophical Magazine and Journal of Science*, 2(11):559–572.

Pedregosa, F., Varoquaux, G., Gramfort, A., Michel, V., Thirion, B., Grisel, O., Blondel, M., Prettenhofer, P., Weiss, R., Dubourg, V., et al. (2011). Scikit-learn: Machine learning in Python. *Journal of machine Learning research*, 12:2825–2830.

Pintard, A. and François, T. (2020). Combining expert knowledge with frequency information to infer CEFR levels for words. In *Proceedings of the 1st Workshop on Tools and Resources to Empower People with REAding DIfficulties (READI)*, pages 85–92.

Rayner, K. and Duffy, S. A. (1986). Lexical complexity and fixation times in reading: Effects of word frequency, verb complexity, and lexical ambiguity. *Memory & cognition*, 14(3):191–201.

Richards, J. C. (1974). Word lists: Problems and prospects. *RELC journal*, 5(2):69–84.

Shardlow, M., Evans, R., Paetzold, G. H., and Zampieri, M. (2021). SemEval-2021 task 1: Lexical complexity prediction. In *Proceedings of the 15th International Workshop on Semantic Evaluation (SemEval-2021)*, pages 1–16, Online, August. Association for Computational Linguistics.

Shardlow, M. (2022). Agree to Disagree: Exploring Subjectivity in Lexical Complexity. In *Proceedings of the 2nd Workshop on Tools and Resources to Empower People with REAding DIfficulties (READI)*.

Strohmaier, D., Gooding, S., Taslimipoor, S., and Kochmar, E. (2020). SeCoDa: Sense complexity dataset. In *Proceedings of the 12th Language Resources and Evaluation Conference*, pages 5962–5967.

Van der Maaten, L. and Hinton, G. (2008). Visualizing data using t-SNE. *Journal of machine learning research*, 9(11).

Wilkens, R., Alfter, D., Wang, X., Pintard, A., Tack, A., Yancey, K., and François, T. (2022). FABRA: French Aggregator-Based Readability Assessment toolkit. In *Proceedings of the thirteenth International Conference on Language Resources and Evaluation (LREC 2022)*.

Yimam, S. M., Biemann, C., Malmasi, S., Paetzold, G., Specia, L., Štajner, S., Tack, A., and Zampieri, M. (2018). A Report on the Complex Word Identification Shared Task 2018. In *Proceedings of the Thirteenth Workshop on Innovative Use of NLP for Building Educational Applications*, pages 66–78, New Orleans, United States. Association for Computational Linguistics.

9. Language Resource References

François, Thomas and Gala, Núria and Watrin, Patrick and Fairon, Cédrick. (2014). *FLELex: a graded lexical resource for French foreign learners*. Proceedings of the Ninth International Conference on Language Resources and Evaluation (LREC'14), ISLRN 742-240-876-017-1.

Sajous, F. and Hathout, N. (2015). GLAWI, a free XML-encoded Machine-Readable Dictionary built from the French Wiktionary. In *Proceedings of the of the eLex 2015 conference*, pages 405–426, Herstmonceux, England, august.

Proceedings of the 2nd READI Workshop @ LREC2022, pages 25–30
Marseille, 24 June 2022

A Multilingual Simplified Language News Corpus

Renate Hauser, Jannis Vamvas, Sarah Ebling, Martin Volk
Department of Computational Linguistics, University of Zurich
renateines.hauser@uzh.ch, {vamvas, ebling, volk}cl.uzh.ch

Abstract

Simplified language news articles are being offered by specialized web portals in several countries. The thousands of articles that have been published over the years are a valuable resource for natural language processing, especially for efforts towards automatic text simplification. In this paper, we present SNIML, a large multilingual corpus of news in simplified language. The corpus contains 13k simplified news articles written in one of six languages: Finnish, French, Italian, Swedish, English, and German. All articles are shared under open licenses that permit academic use. The level of text simplification varies depending on the news portal. We believe that even though SNIML is not a parallel corpus, it can be useful as a complement to the more homogeneous but often smaller corpora of news in the simplified variety of one language that are currently in use.

Keywords: Corpus, Multilinguality, Simplified Language, Accessibility, Text Simplification

1. Introduction

Simplified languages[1] are language varieties that have the purpose of enabling inclusion and social participation of people with low reading competence by making information easier to read and comprehend (Bredel and Maaß, 2016). A typical application domain of simplified language is news articles (Saggion, 2017). In recent years, web portals for simplified news have been created in several languages, and computational approaches to simplified language such as automatic readability assessment or text simplification are gaining interest.

We present SNIML, a corpus of **s**imple **n**ews **i**n **m**any **l**anguages. The corpus contains simplified news articles in Finnish, French, Italian, Swedish, English, and German. It comprises a total of 13,400 articles published between 2003 and 2022. All texts in SNIML are shared under an open license that allows for academic research use. We plan that future news articles are automatically collected and added to the corpus in a temporally stratified way. The corpus and various sub-corpora are available for download.[2]

While some resources for simplified language align simplified versions of texts to standard-language versions, our corpus currently does not contain any news in standard language. Furthermore, the sub-corpora involve texts created according to different simplification guidelines and for different target audiences (Section 3.3). As such, SNIML is particularly useful for automatic readability assessment and for unsupervised, self-supervised or cross-lingual learning. In addition, the simple news articles could be combined with related news articles in standard language, yielding a large-scale multilingual comparable corpus of simple news.

Standard language

One possible difference is that Omicron may be less likely than earlier variants to cause a loss of taste and smell. Research suggests that 48 percent of patients with the original SARS-CoV-2 strain reported loss of smell and 41 percent reported loss of taste, but an analysis of a small Omicron outbreak among vaccinated people in Norway found that only 23 percent of patients reported loss of taste, and only 12 percent reported loss of smell.

Simplified language

Omicron may be less likely to cause a loss of taste and smell. The original virus caused such losses in almost half the sick people, and a study showed less than half that number losing taste and smell with Omicron.

Figure 1: Examples of news text in standard language and simplified language.

2. Related Work

Many previous resources for the computational processing of simplified language are *parallel*, combining a simplified version of a text with its original version. Parallel corpora have been used to train sequence-to-sequence systems for text simplification (Wubben et al. (2012); Nisioi et al. (2017); among others).

Notable examples of parallel corpora include the PorSimples corpus of Brazilian Portuguese news and popular science articles (Aluísio and Gasperin, 2010), the Simplext corpus of Spanish news (Bott and Saggion, 2014), the Newsela corpus of English and Spanish news (Xu et al., 2015), the Alector corpus of French educational texts (Gala et al., 2020), as well as German parallel corpora compiled from various web

[1] The term "simplified language" is used to denote the sum of all "comprehensibility-enhanced varieties of natural languages" (Maaß, 2020, p. 52), i.e., what is commonly termed "Easy Language" (German *leichte Sprache*) and "Plain Language" (German *einfache Sprache*). Maaß (2020, p. 52) mentions "easy-to-understand language" as an umbrella term subsuming these varieties. However, in this contribution, we prefer the term "simplified language" to emphasize the notion of the result of a simplification process.

[2] `https://pub.cl.uzh.ch/projects/sniml/`

sources (Klaper et al., 2013; Battisti et al., 2020). Other parallel news datasets that have been used for automatic simplification in German are the APA dataset (Säuberli et al., 2020) and the 20m dataset (Rios et al., 2021).
Some other previous resources for simplified language are *comparable* corpora, i.e, collections of simplified documents and standard-language documents that share the same topic but are not guaranteed to correlate on the sentence level. For example, Barzilay and Elhadad (2003) combined Encyclopedia Britannica and Britannica Elementary to form a comparable corpus, and they proposed to use alignment techniques to extract parallel sentence pairs. Similarly, the combination of English Wikipedia and Simple English Wikipedia (Zhu et al., 2010), though often treated as a parallel corpus, can be characterized as a comparable corpus, since Simple English entries are not necessarily simplified versions of the standard-language entries. Hwang et al. (2015) used parallel corpus mining methods to create a more parallel version of this dataset. An alternative approach is to extract parallel sentences manually from comparable corpora (Grabar and Cardon, 2018).
The SNIML corpus differs from previous resources with regard to its scale and its rich multilinguality. However, it is neither a parallel nor a comparable corpus, since it currently does not contain standard-language news articles. Thus, the structure of the corpus is best compared to datasets of raw text, such as the CC-News crawl (Common Crawl, 2016) or the Oscar corpus (Centre Inria de Paris, Équipe ALMAnaCH, 2019), even though SNIML is much smaller in size.

3. Corpus

3.1. Data

Language Variety The corpus is a collection of news articles that are written in simplified language. The articles originate from news providers in the USA, Finland (Finnish and Swedish), Belgium (French), Italy, and Switzerland (German). The level of simplification varies between the providers. Also, diverse target groups are addressed by the articles, including people with intellectual disabilities, people with low education, immigrants, emigrants, language learners in general, older adults, and children. The news providers are described in more detail in Section 3.2. Section 3.3 discusses the simplification guidelines involved.

Dataset Statistics Table 1 provides statistics of the corpus and its sub-corpora. The corpus consists of 13,447 articles that were published by the news providers listed below. The lengths of the articles vary greatly, within one provider as well as among the different platforms. *Journal Essentiel* and *Infoeasy* tend to publish longer articles, averaging above 600 tokens per article, while the average for the other providers generally lies below 300 tokens per article.

Temporal Stratification It is planned that news articles continue to be automatically fetched from the web and are added to new versions of the corpus. We plan to release a new version of SNIML every month.

Language	Articles	Sentences	Tokens
Finnish	3,379	41,792	661,194
French (BE)	2,723	102,496	1,759,518
Italian (IT)	2,686	10,824	737,903
Swedish (SV)	2,559	32,145	621,879
English (US)	1,897	50,999	965,805
German (CH)	147	25,964	123,021
Total	13,447	268,350	4,936,181

Table 1: Corpus statistics.

Machine Translations We have created English and German machine translations of most articles. These are mainly intended to be an aid for the users of the web reader interface (Section 4). In addition, the translations could be useful for data augmentation. We provide translations only in cases where the license permits derivative work, namely for articles provided by *Informazione Facile*, *Journal Essentiel* and *The Times in Plain English*.[3]

3.2. News Providers

We collected the articles of six news providers: *Selkosanomat*, *Lätta Bladet*, *Journal Essentiel*, *Informazione Facile*, *The Times in Plain English* and *Infoeasy*. Table 2 gives an overview of the providers and the licenses these providers apply to the text content. Text samples for each provider are listed in the Appendix (Table 3). In what follows, each provider is described in more detail.

3.2.1. Selkosanomat

Selkosanomat is a news platform in Finland that is published by the association Selkokeskus which is part of Kehitysvammaliitto (Developmental Disability Association). It offers a printed magazine as well as a free online newspaper. News on the topics Finland, world, sports, culture, and everyday life are published. The articles are written in Finnish.

3.2.2. Journal Essentiel

Journal Essentiel is an online journal in Belgium that is published by the non-profit association FUNOC (Formation pour l'Unversité ouverte de Charleroi) and primarily aims to be an educational information tool. The articles address current topics and are written in French.

[3] We used the commercial machine translation system of Microsoft Azure Cognitive Services (version 3.0). A manual investigation of the MT quality revealed typical machine translation errors such as wrong pronomina or incorrect gender. While we did not spot translation problems specific to simplified language, future work could investigate this question in more depth.

Provider	URL	Language	License
Selkosanomat	`https://selkosanomat.fi/`	fi	CC BY-NC-ND 4.0
Journal Essentiel	`https://journalessentiel.be/`	fr-BE	CC BY-SA 4.0
Informazione Facile	`https://informazionefacile.it/`	it-IT	CC BY-SA 4.0
Lätta Bladet	`https://ll-bladet.fi/`	sv-SE	CC BY-NC-ND 4.0
The Times in Plain English	`https://www.thetimesinplainenglish.com/`	en-US	*"may be reproduced and distributed by all"*
Infoeasy	`https://infoeasy-news.ch/`	de-CH	CC BY-NC-ND 4.0

Table 2: List of providers of the news articles that constitute the corpus.

3.2.3. Informazione Facile

Informazione Facile is an Italian online news platform published by the non-profit association *IF Informazione Facile*. Many topics are covered by the platform, including international news, Italian news, society and culture, sports, and health.

3.2.4. Lätta Bladet

Lätta Bladet is a sister magazine of *Selkosanomat* that is also situated in Finland and offers articles in Swedish. It is published by Selkokeskus and LL-Center, which is part of the interest organization of Swedish-speaking people with intellectual disabilities in Finland FDUV. Parallel to *Selkosanomat*, a printed magazine as well as a free online newspaper is offered. The same topics are covered by *Lätta Bladet* as by *Selkosanomat*. The articles are written in Swedish.

3.2.5. The Times in Plain English

The Times in Plain English is located in the USA and is published by the *News in Plain English Inc.* A wide range of topics are covered, including international news, news about New York, politics, health and education, law, and economy. To test readability, the publishers use Flesch-Kincaid Grade level (Kincaid et al., 1975).

3.2.6. Infoeasy

Infoeasy is a private initiative in Switzerland that provides an online magazine in easy language. The articles are mainly written in German but an increasing number of articles are translated into French. However, we only used the German articles for this corpus. *Infoeasy* addresses a variety of topics including international news, news about Switzerland, current topics, society, culture, health, sports, economy, and science.

3.3. Simplification Guidelines

In this work, the focus was on creating a corpus of simplified news that is as diverse and comprehensive as possible. The aim was to include texts from sources in several languages and on a broad variety of topics. As a result, also the level of simplification and the target group vary among the different news providers.

Informazione Facile and *The Times in Plain English* assess the complexity of their texts with standardized, length-based readability indices. For assessment, *Informazione Facile* uses the service of *corrige.it* that analyzes texts according to the GULPEASE Index (Lucisano and Piemontese, 1988). The GULPEASE Index is tailored to the Italian language and includes a scale that associates the index with a level of education. The platform states that their texts are suitable for people with reading skills at the level of basic school education. Additionally, *Informazione Facile* uses a basic vocabulary reference (Chiari and Mauro, 2014) to decide which words need further explanation. *The Times in Plain English*, on the other hand, uses the Flesch-Kincaid Grade Level, which assigns a school grade of the U.S. education system that is needed in order to be able to read the text at hand (Kincaid et al., 1975). However, the platform does not state the specific grade level used.

The magazines *Selkosanomat* and *Lätta Bladet* follow the guidelines for plain language that are listed on the website of Selkokeskus.[4]. They include instructions for the vocabulary, such as preferring well-known vocabulary and explaining difficult words, and for the language structure, such as writing short sentences and using active voice. Additionally, specific guidelines for different text types, including media texts, exist. These guidelines are developed and maintained by Selkokeskus.

No information is given by *Infoeasy* and *Journal Essentiel* as to which guidelines they use. Future work could empirically analyze the subcorpora and compare their usefulness for different target audiences.

3.4. Data Collection

To obtain all published articles, we developed web scrapers to scrape the archive pages of the providers. For this, all URLs of the articles were collected. By performing requests to the collected URLs, we obtained the HTML files of the article pages, which we then parsed. In the case of *Informazione Facile*, we received a database export in RSS format of the editors, therefore, no web scraping was needed.

To collect the newly published data, we use an RSS-based web scraping approach. Requests to the RSS feeds of the providers are made daily. The RSS files are parsed to extract the textual data and the metadata. In cases where not all information is contained in the

[4]`https://selkokeskus.fi/selkokieli/`

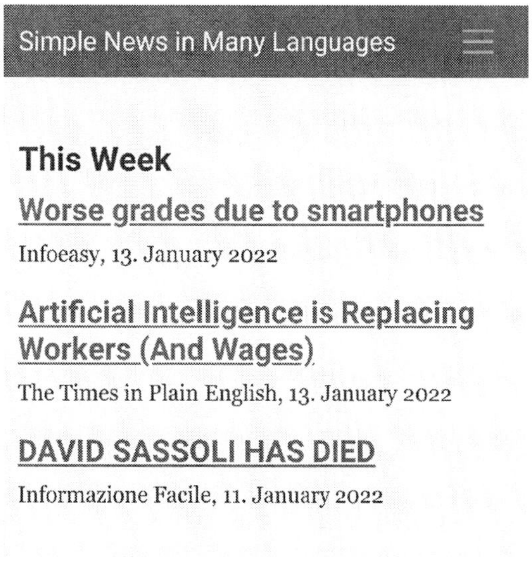

Figure 2: Screenshot of the web reader interface.

RSS file, the web pages of the articles are scraped to obtain the missing data. For each provider, we developed a specialized parser to parse the RSS and HTML files.

3.5. Dataset Format

The corpus is structured in XML. Each article is represented in an article element and can be identified with a unique ID. The textual data consist of the title, a short description and the complete text body of the news article. Additionally, metadata about the article are provided: the category or categories that the article was published in, keywords, the language, the URL, the publication date, the author, and the provider. Providers are further characterized with their name, a link leading to the website, the license, and a link to the license if one exists. As for now, the XML structure does not conform to the TEI format. However, we consider changing the format in a future version of the corpus.
Besides the complete corpus, we provide several sub-corpora. To enable work on only one of the languages, a separate XML file is available for each provider. Also, files containing all articles published in a specific month are provided. For each month, additionally, a sub-corpus for each provider is compiled.

4. Web Reader Interface

In order to make the collected news articles not only available to researchers but also to the target groups of simplified language, we created a web-based reader interface in the style of a news aggregator. The user interface is available in German and English, while the news articles are provided both in their original language and (as machine translations) in the language of the user interface.
The articles are listed with their title, the original news provider, the publication date, and a short description of the content. They are ordered by publication date and are summarized under the week they were published in. The detail view of an article shows its complete text content.

5. Conclusion

The SNIML corpus compiles more than 13k simplified news articles in six languages. The articles are shared under an open license that permits academic use, and are planned to be continually updated.
The SNIML corpus is capable of serving as a useful complement to other resources for simplified language. For example, Simple English Wikipedia has grown very large but is restricted to a single language, text style, and simplification level. Complementing Simple English Wikipedia, the SNIML corpus could thus improve the diversity and multilinguality of language models for simplified language, as well as identification systems for simplified language.
Furthermore, the multilingual composition of SNIML opens up possibilities for the evaluation of cross-lingual transfer. For example, a system for the identification of simplified language could be trained on the English portion and evaluated on the five other languages in the corpus.
Moreover, the temporal stratification of the corpus makes it possible to evaluate a model for simplified language on concepts and topics unseen during training. It has been shown on the example of standard English that temporal generalization is a challenge for language models (Lazaridou et al., 2021), and we believe that it could even more so be a challenge for simplified language.
Future work may consist of aligning the articles to related articles in standard language. Such an extended version of SNIML could offer new opportunities for parallel corpus mining, or even for experiments towards an unsupervised text simplification system.

6. Acknowledgements

We thank the providers of the news articles in the corpus, namely *The Times in Plain English*, *Selkosanomat* and *Lätta Bladet*, *Journal Essentiel*, *Informazione Facile*, and *Infoeasy*, for agreeing to make their work available under an open license.

7. Bibliographical References

Aluísio, S. and Gasperin, C. (2010). Fostering digital inclusion and accessibility: The PorSimples project for simplification of Portuguese texts. In *Proceedings of the NAACL HLT 2010 Young Investigators Workshop on Computational Approaches to Languages of the Americas*, pages 46–53, Los Angeles,

California, June. Association for Computational Linguistics.

Barzilay, R. and Elhadad, N. (2003). Sentence alignment for monolingual comparable corpora. In *Proceedings of the 2003 Conference on Empirical Methods in Natural Language Processing*, pages 25–32.

Battisti, A., Pfütze, D., Säuberli, A., Kostrzewa, M., and Ebling, S. (2020). A corpus for automatic readability assessment and text simplification of German. In *Proceedings of the 12th Language Resources and Evaluation Conference*, pages 3302–3311, Marseille, France, May. European Language Resources Association.

Bott, S. and Saggion, H. (2014). Text simplification resources for Spanish. *Language Resources and Evaluation*, 48(1):93–120, March.

Bredel, U. and Maaß, C. (2016). *Leichte Sprache. Theoretische Grundlagen. Orientierung für die Praxis.* Dudenverlag, Berlin.

Chiari, I. and Mauro, T. (2014). The new basic vocabulary of Italian as a linguistic resource. In *First Italian Conference on Computational Linguistics CLiC-it 2014*, pages 113–116, 10.

Gala, N., Tack, A., Javourey-Drevet, L., François, T., and Ziegler, J. C. (2020). Alector: A parallel corpus of simplified French texts with alignments of misreadings by poor and dyslexic readers. In *Proceedings of the 12th Language Resources and Evaluation Conference*, pages 1353–1361, Marseille, France, May. European Language Resources Association.

Grabar, N. and Cardon, R. (2018). CLEAR – simple corpus for medical French. In *Proceedings of the 1st Workshop on Automatic Text Adaptation (ATA)*, pages 3–9, Tilburg, the Netherlands, November. Association for Computational Linguistics.

Hwang, W., Hajishirzi, H., Ostendorf, M., and Wu, W. (2015). Aligning sentences from standard Wikipedia to Simple Wikipedia. In *Proceedings of the 2015 Conference of the North American Chapter of the Association for Computational Linguistics: Human Language Technologies*, pages 211–217, Denver, Colorado, May–June. Association for Computational Linguistics.

Kincaid, J. P., Fishburne Jr, R. P., Rogers, R. L., and Chissom, B. S. (1975). Derivation of new readability formulas (automated readability index, fog count and flesch reading ease formula) for navy enlisted personnel. Technical report, Naval Technical Training Command Millington TN Research Branch.

Klaper, D., Ebling, S., and Volk, M. (2013). Building a German/simple German parallel corpus for automatic text simplification. In *Proceedings of the Second Workshop on Predicting and Improving Text Readability for Target Reader Populations*, pages 11–19, Sofia, Bulgaria, August. Association for Computational Linguistics.

Lazaridou, A., Kuncoro, A., Gribovskaya, E., Agrawal, D., Liska, A., Terzi, T., Gimenez, M., de Masson d'Autume, C., Kocisky, T., Ruder, S., et al. (2021). Mind the gap: Assessing temporal generalization in neural language models. *Advances in Neural Information Processing Systems*, 34.

Lucisano, P. and Piemontese, M. E. (1988). Gulpease: una formula per la predizione della difficoltà dei testi in lingua italiana. *Scuola e città*, 3(31):110–124.

Maaß, C. (2020). *Easy Language – Plain Language – Easy Language Plus. Balancing Comprehensibility and Acceptability*, volume 3 of *Easy – Plain – Accessible*. Frank & Timme.

Nisioi, S., Štajner, S., Ponzetto, S. P., and Dinu, L. P. (2017). Exploring neural text simplification models. In *Proceedings of the 55th Annual Meeting of the Association for Computational Linguistics (Volume 2: Short Papers)*, pages 85–91, Vancouver, Canada, July. Association for Computational Linguistics.

Rios, A., Spring, N., Kew, T., Kostrzewa, M., Säuberli, A., Müller, M., and Ebling, S. (2021). A new dataset and efficient baselines for document-level text simplification in German. In *Proceedings of the Third Workshop on New Frontiers in Summarization*, pages 152–161, Online and in Dominican Republic, November. Association for Computational Linguistics.

Saggion, H. (2017). *Automatic Text Simplification.* Morgan & Claypool Publishers.

Säuberli, A., Ebling, S., and Volk, M. (2020). Benchmarking data-driven automatic text simplification for German. In *Proceedings of the 1st Workshop on Tools and Resources to Empower People with REAding DIfficulties (READI)*, pages 41–48, Marseille, France, May. European Language Resources Association.

Wubben, S., van den Bosch, A., and Krahmer, E. (2012). Sentence simplification by monolingual machine translation. In *Proceedings of the 50th Annual Meeting of the Association for Computational Linguistics (Volume 1: Long Papers)*, pages 1015–1024, Jeju Island, Korea, July. Association for Computational Linguistics.

Xu, W., Callison-Burch, C., and Napoles, C. (2015). Problems in Current Text Simplification Research: New Data Can Help. *Transactions of the Association for Computational Linguistics*, 3:283–297, 05.

Zhu, Z., Bernhard, D., and Gurevych, I. (2010). A monolingual tree-based translation model for sentence simplification. In *Proceedings of the 23rd International Conference on Computational Linguistics (Coling 2010)*, pages 1353–1361, Beijing, China, August. Coling 2010 Organizing Committee.

8. Language Resource References

Centre Inria de Paris, Équipe ALMAnaCH. (2019). *OSCAR*.

Common Crawl. (2016). *CC-News*.

Appendix

Provider	Example	English machine translation
The Times in Plain English	With Omicron, you may get a scratchy throat, nasal congestion, a dry cough, and muscle pain in the lower back. These are the same symptoms as the Delta variant, and they are also the symptoms of the first coronavirus outbreak. An expert said, "It is still too early to say there is any difference in the Omicron symptoms."	-
Selkosanomat	Rokotuksia halutaan vauhdittaa, koska koronaviruksen uusi muunnos omikron leviää yhä nopeammin. Britanniassa, Tanskassa ja Norjassa omikron on levinnyt laajemmin kuin Suomessa. Näissä maissa suunnitellaan uusia tiukkoja rajoituksia.	-
Journal Essentiel	Je comprends les personnes qui disent: "Nous ne savons pas ce que ces vaccins pourraient nous causer à l'avenir." J'ai envie de leur répondre: "Il y a sans doute certains effets à long terme qui sont inconnus mais aujourd'hui, le vaccin est notre meilleur moyen pour sortir de cette pandémie."	*I understand people who say, "We don't know what these vaccines might do to us in the future." I want to answer them: "There are probably some long-term effects that are unknown but today, the vaccine is our best way out of this pandemic."*
Informazione Facile	• I bambini fino agli 11 anni riceveranno un terzo della dose prevista sopra i 12 anni. • La sperimentazione del vaccino è stata fatta su un piccolo numero di bambini: 2.300.	• *Children up to the age of 11 will receive one third of the expected dose over the age of 12.* • *The vaccine trial was done on a small number of children: 2,300,*
Lätta Bladet	Regeringen vill få fart på vaccineringen. I Finland finns det fortfarande ungefär 800 000 vuxna som inte har fått coronavaccin. Regeringen har också bestämt att man nu börjar vaccinera barn över 5 år mot corona.	-
Infoeasy	Genesen ist ein anderes Wort für: wieder gesund. Wir brauchen darum jetzt an vielen Orten ein Covid-Zertifikat. Nur mit dem Zertifikat dürfen wir hinein. Und dieses Zertifikat bekommen nur Personen, • die geimpft sind. • die genesen sind. • die einen Corona-Test gemacht haben. Und der Test muss negativ sein.[5]	*Recovery is another word for: healthy again.* *That's why we now need a Covid certificate in many places.* *We are only allowed in with the certificate.* *And this certificate is only given to people* • *those who are vaccinated.* • *that have recovered.* • *who have taken a corona test. And the test must be negative.*

Table 3: Text examples for each news provider. Machine translations are provided if the license permits derivative work.

Proceedings of the 2nd READI Workshop @ LREC2022, pages 31–38
Marseille, 24 June 2022

The Swedish Simplification Toolkit: Designed with Target Audiences in Mind

Evelina Rennes, Marina Santini, Arne Jönsson
Linköping University, RISE, Linköping University
Linköping, Sweden, Stockholm, Sweden, Linköping, Sweden
evelina.rennes@liu.se, marina.santini@ri.se, arne.jonsson@liu.se

Abstract

In this paper, we present the current version of *The Swedish Simplification Toolkit*. The toolkit includes computational and empirical tools that have been developed along the years to explore a still neglected area of NLP, namely the simplification of "standard" texts to meet the needs of target audiences. Target audiences, such as people affected by dyslexia, aphasia, autism, but also children and second language learners, require different types of text simplification and adaptation. For example, while individuals with aphasia have difficulties in reading compounds (such as *arbetsmarknadsdepartement*, eng. ministry of employment), second language learners struggle with cultural-specific vocabulary (e.g. *konfliktrádd*, eng. afraid of conflicts). The toolkit allows user to selectively select the types of simplification that meet the specific needs of the target audience they belong to. The Swedish Simplification Toolkit is one of the first attempts to overcome the one-fits-all approach that is still dominant in Automatic Text Simplification, and proposes a set of computational methods that, used individually or in combination, may help individuals reduce reading (and writing) difficulties.

Keywords: automatic text simplification, easy-to-read, automatic text adaptation

1. Introduction

Poor readers come in many forms and include those affected by cognitive disabilities (e.g. individuals with dyslexia), but also those who have not yet developed the skills to master the language (e.g. children and second language learners). Poor readers from these different target groups have more or less widespread cognitive and language difficulties which selectively impair different aspects of reading comprehension. To meet the demands of accessible text of poor readers, a number of initiatives have attempted to adapt texts and make them more comprehensible. Examples of such initiatives in Sweden are the recommendations issued by The Swedish Agency for Accessible Media (Swedish: Myndigheten för tillgängliga medier, (MTM, 2021) MTM and the initiative "Comprehensible text" (Swedish: Begriplig text) (Begriplig Text, 2019). Internationally, the most influential set of guidelines on Easy Language is Plain text (PLAIN, 2011). Such recommendations and guidelines commonly have a one-size-fits-all approach, which means that they have a generalist approach and sometimes overlook the factors underlying different types of reading difficulties. It has been already been pointed out that recommendations and guidelines are often based on common sense assumptions rather than empirical testing on groups of poor readers (Wengelin, 2015).

Although the one-size-fits-all approach is an important first step, individuals who struggle with reading have deficits in cognitive and language skills which make their reading process qualitatively different. Therefore, it is essential to consider the different target audiences when developing recommendations and guidelines, but also when implementing Automatic Text Simplification (ATS) systems. The readers' needs cannot, and should not, be taken out of the equation, rather their needs should be the cornerstone of ATS.

The rationale of the *Swedish Simplification Toolkit* is then to start addressing the one-fits-all bias that still exists in Automatic Text Simplification by putting the linguistic needs of the target audience in the limelight. The set of computational methods underpinning the toolkit address some of these needs and at the same time reflects the current state-of-the-art in ATS for the Swedish language.

The toolkit is the concrete answer to the two research questions that drive our work, namely:

1. What types of linguistic simplification are needed, and which ones are implementable for the Swedish language?
2. Can ATS be conceived, designed and implemented to meet the needs of different target audiences?

In the next sections, we provide the background and illustrate our approach that we have implemented for the Swedish language.

2. Profiling Selected Target Audiences

In the short description of the target audiences provided below, we single out different linguistic phenomena that can be used to characterise audience-specific simplification needs. Simplification may be needed at lexical level (e.g. for individuals with dyslexia), at syntactic levels (e.g. for the individuals affected by aphasia) or at discourse levels (e.g. for people with Autism Spectrum Disorder). Table 1 summarizes the target audiences and their main simplification needs.

Dyslexia. In the International Statistical Classification of Diseases and Related Health Problems - Eleventh

Table 1: Target audiences and their simplification needs

	Lexical Simpification	Syntactic Simplification	Discourse-level Simplification
Dyslexia	Long words Less frequent words Homophones Words that are orthographically similar New words Non-words		
Aphasia	Information density Noun compounds	Long sentences Long sequences of adjectives Passive voice Object relative clauses Comparison of word meaning	
Intellectual Disability (ID)	Limited vocabulary		
Deaf and Hard-of-Hearing	Limited vocabulary	Complex sentences Morphology Syntax	
Austism Spectrum Disorder	Words related to emotions		Figurative language Texts that require little social knowledge
Second Language Learners	Limited vocabulary		Tight text structure
Children	New words Limited vocabulary		

Revision (ICD-11), developmental dyslexia is categorised under F81.0 Specific reading disorder. An article discussing the major findings of the research on dyslexia during the last decades (Vellutino et al., 2004) showed that word identification inadequacies were the most basic cause of reading difficulties. Individuals with dyslexia experience a wide range of difficulties, such as problems with long words and less frequent words (Hyönä and Olson, 1995; Rello et al., 2013). Except for long and unfamiliar words, other issues that individuals with dyslexia may encounter have been listed, such as homophones, words that are orthographically similar, new words, and nonwords (Rello et al., 2013).

Aphasia is a language impairment caused by brain damage acquired by for example stroke, trauma to the head, neuro-degenerative diseases or brain surgery. Common difficulties experience by individuals with aphasia include high information density, long sentences, long sequences of adjectives, passive voice and noun compounds (Carroll et al., 1999). Other difficulties described in the literature are sentences with object relative clauses and comparisons of word meaning ("is x larger than y?") (Hillis, 2007).

Intellectual disability (ID) is characterised by low IQ and limitations in many cognitive abilities, such as working memory and executive functions (Danielsson et al., 2012). Individuals with ID have a delay in reading as compared to typical readers which is manifested in capabilities concerning decoding and reading comprehension (Nilsson et al., 2021b; Nilsson et al., 2021a). Using simple texts in order to enhance reading skills is a common strategy in education targeting individuals with ID. Due to the limited amount of textual resources, the teachers face a challenge when choosing accurate educational material, and they often adapt the texts themselves, for example by the use of readability metrics and metrics for reading level estimation, or by writing completely new texts.

Deaf and Hard-of-Hearing. One group of people that may struggle with reading is the deaf or hard-of-hearing. It is established that childhood hearing loss deeply affects language development, and the language deficits may also affect other cognitive developmental areas related to language negatively, such as the development of literacy (Lederberg et al., 2013). Children that are deaf and hard-of-hearing especially struggle with grammar (ibid.), most prominently syntactically complex sentences (Siddharthan, 2003) and grammatical morphology, as well as a limited vocabulary (Fabbretti et al., 1998).

Autism Spectrum Disorder (ASD). With respect to reading comprehension skills, the ASD audience is diverse. The reading difficulties are less straightforward to describe than those exhibited in most of the other target audiences, due to the large variety of symptoms included in the diagnosis. Difficulties understanding figurative language is one of the most prominent problems. According to a meta-analysis of the research on figurative language for individuals with ASD (Kalandadze et al., 2018), the difficulties seem to be related to basic language skills, and that enhanced general language skills might improve the comprehension of figurative language. The authors highlighted that it is important for individuals with ASD to be exposed to figurative language, and that it is beneficial to provide explanations to such constructions instead of avoiding them. A meta-analysis of reading comprehension skills of individuals with ASD found that the performance on reading comprehension of individuals with ASD depend on text type (Brown et al., 2013). Generally, individuals with ASD perform better when reading texts that require little social knowledge. However, they also highlighted the fact that ASD covers a variety of symptoms and deficits, and that the diagnosis in itself does not imply any reading comprehension difficulties.

Second Language Learners. This audience differs from many of the other groups, since learners of a new language do not necessarily have any impairment that hinders reading or understanding, but may rather experience difficulties related to a poor vocabulary, unfamiliarity of specific cultural phenomena, or a lack of knowledge about the grammar of the language that is being learnt. Knowing a language's vocabulary has proved to be an important factor for learning a new language. Knowing a language's vocabulary has proved to be an important factor for learning a new language.

Children. Although not having any physical or cognitive disability, a possible target audience for text adaptation or simplification is children. As the Internet is becoming the dominating source of textual information, there is a growing need for text adapted to the reading level of children of different ages. There is a developmental aspect of children's reading that should not be disregarded. The text should not be too simple, since reading encourages learning of new words, and the reading level should thus be adapted to the reading level of the certain reader (De Belder and Moens, 2010).

3. Simplification techniques

In this section we briefly present techniques that address the different levels of simplification.

Lexical simplification refers to the automatic simplification at word level. It aims at identifying and replacing complex words (or phrases) by an easier-to-read alternative. Regardless of how we define simple words, the substitution of words that are more complex to simpler words with the same meaning is a rather well-studied area in ATS (e.g. (Paetzold and Specia, 2017) for an overview), and although it is a challenging task with many non-trivial subtasks (identifying complex words, disambiguating word senses, etc.), the guidelines of substituting complex words and compounds can be considered possible to automate. The avoidance of jargon and technical terms can be solved with specialised term lists, such as the black list (Stadsrådsberedningen) used by the Swedish public authorities. To not split words on two lines, and how to write (or not write) numerical expressions are other guidelines that are relatively easy to automate. Abbreviations should be avoided and this is also a task that can be automated.

Syntactic simplification refers to the automatic simplification at text level. It aims at simplifying the text by restructuring the words of the sentences, and/or rewriting it into smaller sentences. The issue of keeping the text brief can be addressed through different kinds of ATS. For example, superfluous words and phrases can be recognised and deleted. Such simplification operations have been previously identified for Swedish Easy Language text (Decker, 2003), and while operations like these are relatively simple to implement from a technical point of view, one must be aware of the risk that relevant text information might be deleted in the process, which could cause confusion or impair the experienced reading flow of the reader. One guideline is to keep one proposition per sentence. To follow this guideline is slightly more complicated, as it requires some semantic parsing. One possible solution to this could be event-based simplification (see for example (Štajner et al., 2016)), that identifies mentions of factual events and delete sentences or parts of sentences that are irrelevant to these event mentions. Such simplification approaches could enhance text comprehension by deleting irrelevant information and highlighting the main information, but will naturally also result in some loss of information. It is clear that the deletion of words, phrases or information could result in a more readable text, but there is also a risk that that the resulting text is, in fact, less readable. This could be due to loss of core information, as described above, but it could also be due to more typographic reasons, i.e. that features of the text layout makes the text less appealing to read. One guideline suggests to mix long and short sentences. This could be considered as a parameter when applying guidelines that intend to write as brief as possible. Guidelines that change negative statements to positive statements are possible to automate, but require a mechanism for identifying such structures, as well as a set of rewriting suggestions. For relatively simple cases (PLAIN, 2011), the task is more or less analogous to lexical simplification, but for more complicated cases with, for example, double negations, the task is slightly more complex. Some work has been done on identifying and substituting negations within the medical domain (Burgers et al., 2015; Mukherjee et al., 2017). It is generally recommended to use personal pronouns, and to address the reader directly. Such linguistic simplification strategies have previously been, at least partially, implemented in a rule-based simplification system (Rennes and Jönsson, 2015). In the same system, a rule for reordering sentences so that they keep a straight word order, with subject, verb and object kept close to each other, was implemented.

Discourse-level simplification. Syntactic skills facilitate access of meaning from grammatical structures, which is a fundamental process in gaining text meaning at any level of reading comprehension. Discourse skills allow readers to understand the cohesive interlinks within and between sentences and is important for a macro level of passage understanding. The macro level simplification could be easily implemented in an ATS tool with existing techniques. For example, to make the main information easy to find could include the automatic extraction of keywords and present them in clear ways (boldface, headlines, bullet lists, etc.), as well as providing an automatic summary of the text (Hahn and Mani, 2000). Keyword extraction and extractive summarisation (to extract the most important sentences of a text) are techniques that could be relatively easily implemented, whereas abstractive summarisation (to rewrite the summary from scratch) require more sophisticated methods and data for training (Monsen and Jönsson, 2021). The guideline to let the general and the most important information be presented in the beginning could possibly be approached using the same keyword extraction and summarisation techniques.

4. The Swedish Simplification Toolkit

The Swedish Simplification Toolkit is a modular text simplification system covering a wide range of simplification and summarization functions. It is important to point out that in this context summarization is used as simplification tools as explained in Smith and Jönsson (2011a).

The Swedish Simplification Toolkit can be used via two interfaces that offer complementary functions, namely FRIENDLYREADER (more targeted to reading) and TECST (more targeted to writing), see Figure 1.

Both FRIENDLYREADER and TECST leverage on four modules: STILLETT (Rennes and Jönsson, 2015), TEXTCOMP (Falkenjack, 2018; Falkenjack et al., 2013), COGSUM (Smith and Jönsson, 2011a; Smith and Jönsson, 2011b) and JULIUSUM (Monsen and Jönsson, 2021). SAPIS (Fahlborg and Rennes, 2016; Falkenjack et al., 2017) is a REST API aiming to make the services readily available and is used by both FRIENDLYREADER and TECST. All the core modules have been evaluated according to the criteria of intrinsic evaluation and all results can be found in the references given below.

In the rest of the section, first we describe the core modules and than the user interfaces through which the core modules are deployed.

STILLETT (Rennes and Jönsson, 2015) is a rule-based automatic text simplification tool for Swedish. It started off as a Java application, partly built on COGFLUX (Rybing et al., 2010), with a dynamic structure of processes and modules, where each process runs a number of modules. In its original implementation, STILLETT included rules for rewriting to passive-to-active, quotation inversion, rearranging to straight word order, sentence split, and synonym replacement, in addition to the original rule sets proposed by Decker (2003). The synonym replacement module implemented in STILLETT originally combined the word pairs from the Synlex lexicon (Kann, 2004) and frequency information. The Synlex lexicon includes 82,000 word pairs including an annotation of level of synonymity. This score was calculated by ratings made by voluntary Internet users, who graded the synonym pairs based on how synonymous they were. In addition to these strategies, we developed and evaluated other methods for finding more comprehensible synonyms. The first method was based on a corpus of texts in simple Swedish, and the other method was based on theories from the field of cognitive linguistics where hypernyms with characteristics of basic-level words were found to be useful for the task of lexical simplification (Rennes and Jönsson, 2021).

STILLETT has undergone several improvements (see for instance Johansson and Rennes (2016)) since the first implementation and is today built on Python3, and uses dep_tregex 1(Dvorkovich et al., 2016), for reordering the dependency trees using rules inspired by Tregex (Levy and Andrew, 2006). The included rule set still contains the original rules for rewriting to passive-to-active, quotation inversion, rearranging to straight word order, and sentence split, but the rules are further refined. The preprocessor is accessed through the REST API SAPIS and runs the Swedish pipeline with EFSELAB (Östling, 2018) and MaltParser (Nivre et al., 2007) version 1.9.0.

TEXTCOMP is a collection of text complexity measures. The main part of the included measures consists of the SCREAM (Swedish Compound READability Metric) features (Sjöholm, 2012). SCREAM features include surface, lexical and structural features (the complete list of SCREAM features can be found in Falkenjack (2018) and Falkenjack et al. (2013)). More recently, cohesion-related measures have been included, namely the Coh-Metrix measurements, translated to Swedish from the orginal English version (Graesser et al., 2004).

COGSUM (Smith and Jönsson, 2011a; Smith and Jönsson, 2011b) is an automatic extractive summariser, which means that it extracts the most important sentences in order to create a shorter version of the text. COGSUM uses the Random Indexing (RI) (Hassel, 2011; Hassel, 2007) word space model with pre-trained word vectors, and a modified version of the PageRank algorithm to rank the sentences (Chatterjee and Mohan, 2007). Evaluations have shown that COGSUM performs at an average ROUGE-1 score of 0.6.

JULIUSUM (Monsen and Jönsson, 2021) is an automatic abstractive summariser. An abstractive summarisation differs from an extractive summarisation in that the words and sentences are not directly extracted from the text, but instead generated based on a pre-trained model. This means that abstractive summaries can contain completely novel words and sentences not present in the source text, while maintaining the key content of the text. JULIUSUM was trained utilising the methodology proposed by Rothe et al. (2020), using a pre-trained Swedish BERT model (Malmsten et al., 2020) to warm-start an encoder-decoder model. The data used for training consisted of news articles published in Sweden's largest morning newspaper Dagens Nyheter (DN) during the years 2000–2020.

FRIENDLYREADER, Figure 1 left, is a customizable interface that can be adjusted to the specific needs of different target audiences. The idea is that the interface should contain the entire palette of simplification techniques, including both linguistic and layout simplifications, and that the user can adapt the text completely to their individual needs. FRIENDLYREADER is under constant development. In addition to the modules for simplification and summarization, FRIENDLYREADER also contains text-to-speech functionality, which lets the reader listen to the text. The simplification related to text layout is the possibility to change font size, line spacing, font and line length. In its current state, the user pastes the text into a large text field and presses Run. The view in the left of Figure 1 is then presented to the user. The layout consists of three parts. The main field is the middle field, where the the text is presented to the reader. The left-hand side contains a menu with various types of text simplification. The user is presented with a number of options: 1. Summarise: The user can summarise the text using a slider that outputs summaries of different lengths. 2. Simplify: The user can simplify the text using the syntactic simplification operations of STILLETT. There are check boxes that lets the user choose what operations to make, and the rules are applied directly to the text. 3. Synonyms: By clicking Synonyms, the user can activate the exhibition of synonyms of words in the text. Words with available synonyms are highlighted in the text, and by clicking any such word, the user is presented to a list of possible synonyms. 4. Text-to-speech: The user can have the text read out loud by activating the text-to-speech functionality. 5. Text complexity: The user can see basic text complexity measures, such as LIX and OVIX. The user is also presented to a visualisation of the complexity of the text presented in a radar chart. The right-hand side contains a menu with various simplification options related to text visualization.

TECST (Text Complexity and Simplification Toolkit), Figure 1 right, is a a tool developed for web editors and writers of easy language texts, but could be used by anyone interested in calculating the complexity of a text, as well as applying various text simplification techniques. The intuition behind this tool is that providing the easy language text writers with advanced techniques for measuring and visualising complexity, identifying complex linguistic structures, and give advice on how such structures should be adapted to suit the needs of various target audiences, is one way of making the text simplification process quicker and cheaper, without overlooking the expertise and unique competence provided by the human writer.
The TECST layout, presented in the right of Figure 1, consists of two fields: the editor, which makes up the main part of the tool layout, and the simplification and visualisation field. The editor allows the writer to customise the text using different fonts, font sizes, bold face, bullet point lists, and similar features often included in text editing tools. The simplification and visualisation field, on the right-hand side, presents information regarding the current complexity and simplification suggestions of the text. It has three tabs: visualisation, text information and text simplification. In the visualisaton tab, a text complexity visualisation in the form of a radar chart is presented. In the text information tab, the writer can choose to see a summary of the text, as well as some general information about the current text, such as the text length in words and sentences, as well as a subset of the text complexity measures. Similarly to the features presented in the visualisation, the subset of text complexity features shown under the text information tab is customisable. The third tab, text simplification, allows the writer to make adaptations to the text. There are four options here.
Summarisation: The user can summarise the text, by the use of a slider that regulates the length of the resulting summary. 2. Synonyms: The user can use a check box to highlight the words of the text that have available synonyms, and customise the synonym replacement functionality to mark long words, i.e. words longer than some length chosen by the user. 3. Markings: The user can use check boxes to let the tool identify and highlight different features of the text, such as long words, long sentences, and numbers. The number of characters that make up a long word is customisable, as well as the number of words that make up a long sentence. 4. Text simplification suggestions: The user can get suggested simplifications of complex sentences.

5. Discussion

The Swedish Simplification Toolkit meets the needs of the target audiences described in Section 2. There is a close match between the characterization of target audience presented in Table 1 and the options provided in the user interfaces. For example, in FRIENDLYREADER, people affected by ID, as well as non-native speakers and children, can click the button "Visa Synonymer" (Show synonyms) to fill up the gap of their limited vocabulary. People affected by aphasia have the possibility to convert passive voice into active voice by checking the box "passiv till aktiv form" (pas-

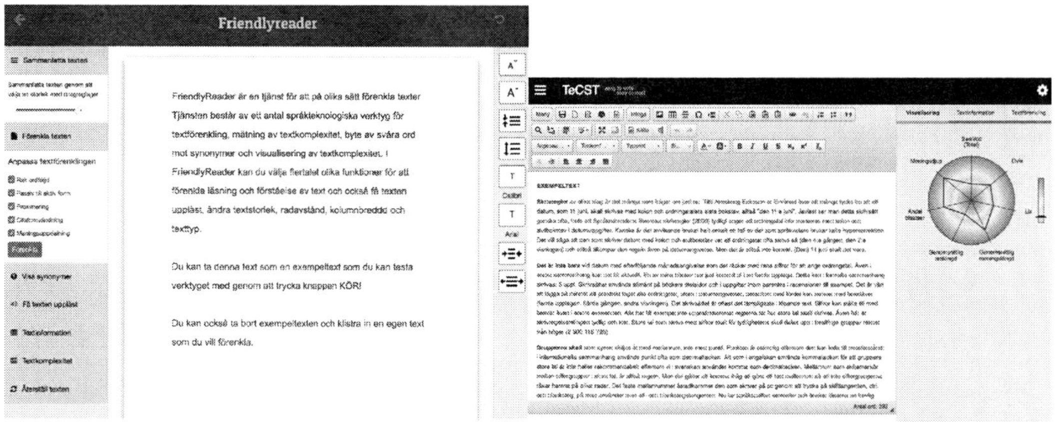

Figure 1: FRIENDLYREADER, left and TECST, right

sive to active form). The aphasic can also shorten long sentences that are difficult for the to process by using the summarization functions. In TECST, it is possible to visualize the spikes of the complexity of a text via a radar chart and then decide what types of simplifications needed. For instance, people with dyslexia might decide to choose shorter synonyms of long words, but leave the syntactic complexity untouched since this type of complexity does not hinder their reading comprehension.

At the time of this publication, no options have been implemented to convert figurative language into de-metaphorized language. Also, no functionality has been created yet to compensate for the social knowledge that autistic people might miss from a standard text.

As mentioned above, the core modules have been evaluated, but the usability of the toolkit has not yet been tested on target audiences. Such evaluations include two activities, to assess the interface and interaction with the various simplification tools, and assessment of the various simplification techniques and text complexity measures.

The latter is currently done in three studies, one involving students with dyslexia, one involving students having an intellectual disability and one with teachers for students with reading difficulties. The first two studies use texts that are adapted using the toolkit. The students read them on paper and assess the usability from various perspectives. The study with teachers investigate the use of text complexity measures and visualisation of text complexity and is conducted in focus groups where the teachers are presented a variety of text complexity measures and visualisations. The reason for using paper and not the interface is, of course, that we want to focus on the usability of the techniques for text simplification and complexity measure, not the usability of the interface.

The answers to the research questions are:

1. What types of linguistic simplification are needed, and which ones are implementable for the Swedish language?

   Answer: lexical, syntactic and discourse level simplification are needed for the target audiences that we have explored in this paper. However for the Swedish language, many areas are unexplored, as seen from the empty cells in Table 1, especially for discourse-level simplification.

2. Can ATS be conceived, designed and implemented to meet the needs of different target audiences?

   Answer: Absolutely yes. We have presented an approach (core modules + interfaces) that shows how target audiences can adapt standard text to their needs.

6. Conclusion and Future Work

In this paper we presented the Swedish Simplification Toolkit, conceived and designed with the target audiences in mind. The toolkit is the outcome of years of theoretical and computational research. However, much remains to be done. Our next step will be the validation of the adaptations on readers from the target audiences. We are currently testing the effects of specific simplification operations on individuals with dyslexia and intellectual disabilities, and the results of this study will provide a starting point for further development of more customized text simplification. Future work includes the validation of the usability of the interfaces directly by target audiences.

7. Acknowledgements

This work has been funded by The Swedish Research Council (VR) and Sweden's innovation agency (VINOVA).

8. References

Begriplig Text. (2019). *19 råd för att skriva begripligt.* Dyslexiförbundet.

Brown, H. M., Oram-Cardy, J., and Johnson, A. (2013). A meta-analysis of the reading comprehension skills of individuals on the autism spectrum. *Journal of Autism and Developmental Disorders*, 43(4):932–955.

Burgers, C., Beukeboom, C. J., Sparks, L., and Diepeveen, V. (2015). How (not) to inform patients about drug use: use and effects of negations in dutch patient information leaflets. *Pharmacoepidemiology and drug safety*, 24(2):137–143.

Carroll, J., Minnen, G., Pearce, D., Canning, Y., Devlin, S., and Tait, J. (1999). Simplifying Text for Language-Impaired Readers. In *Proceedings of the 9th Conference of the European Chapter of the Association for Computational Linguistics (EACL)*, pages 269–270.

Chatterjee, N. and Mohan, S. (2007). Extraction-Based Single-Document Summarization Using Random Indexing. In *Proceedings of the 19th IEEE international Conference on Tools with Artificial intelligence – (ICTAI 2007)*, pages 448–455.

Danielsson, H., Henry, L., Messer, D., and Rönnberg, J. (2012). Strengths and weaknesses in executive functioning in children with intellectual disability. *Research in developmental disabilities*, 33(2):600–607.

De Belder, J. and Moens, M.-F. (2010). Text simplification for children. In *Proceedings of the SIGIR workshop on accessible search systems*, pages 19–26. ACM; New York.

Decker, A. (2003). Towards automatic grammatical simplification of Swedish text. Master's thesis, Stockholm University.

Dvorkovich, A., Gubanov, S., and Galinskaya, I. (2016). Yandex School of Data Analysis approach to English-Turkish translation at WMT16 News Translation Task. In *Proceedings of the First Conference on Machine Translation*, volume 2, pages 281–288, Berlin, Germany.

Fabbretti, D., Volterra, V., and Pontecorvo, C. (1998). Written language abilities in deaf italians. *The Journal of Deaf Studies and Deaf Education*, 3(3):231–244.

Fahlborg, D. and Rennes, E. (2016). Introducing SAPIS - an API service for text analysis and simplification. In *The second national Swe-Clarin workshop: Research collaborations for the digital age, Umeå, Sweden.*

Falkenjack, J., Heimann Mühlenbock, K., and Jönsson, A. (2013). Features Indicating Readability in Swedish Text. In *Proceedings of the 19th Nordic Conference of Computational Linguistics (NoDaLiDa-2013), Oslo, Norway*, number 085 in NEALT Proceedings Series 16, pages 27–40. Linköping University Electronic Press.

Falkenjack, J., Rennes, E., Fahlborg, D., Johansson, V., and Jönsson, A. (2017). Services for text simplification and analysis. In *Proceedings of the 21st Nordic Conference on Computational Linguistics, Gothemburg, Sweden.*

Falkenjack, J. (2018). *Towards a model of general text complexity for Swedish.* Licentiate thesis, Linköping University Electronic Press.

Graesser, A. C., McNamara, D. S., Louwerse, M. M., and Cai, Z. (2004). Coh-metrix: Analysis of text on cohesion and language. *Behavior research methods, instruments, & computers*, 36(2):193–202.

Hahn, U. and Mani, I. (2000). The Challenges of Automatic Summarization. *Computer*, 33(11):29–36.

Hassel, M. (2007). *Resource Lean and Portable Automatic Text Summarization.* Ph.D. thesis, ISRN-KTH/CSC/A–07/09-SE, KTH, Sweden.

Hassel, M. (2011). Java Random Indexing toolkit, 1. `http://www.csc.kth.se/~xmartin/java/`.

Hillis, A. E. (2007). Aphasia: Progress in the last quarter of a century. *Neurology*, 69:200–213.

Hyönä, J. and Olson, R. K. (1995). Eye fixation patterns among dyslexic and normal readers: Effects of word length and word frequency. *Journal of Experimental Psychology: Learning, Memory, and Cognition*, 21(6):1430.

Johansson, V. and Rennes, E. (2016). Automatic extraction of synonyms from an easy-to-read corpus. In *Proceedings of the Sixth Swedish Language Technology Conference (SLTC-16), Umeå, Sweden.*

Kalandadze, T., Norbury, C., Nærland, T., and Næss, K.-A. B. (2018). Figurative language comprehension in individuals with autism spectrum disorder: A meta-analytic review. *Autism*, 22(2):99–117.

Kann, V. (2004). Folkets användning av Lexin – en resurs. In *Lexinkonferens 2004*, Stockholm, Sweden.

Lederberg, A. R., Schick, B., and Spencer, P. E. (2013). Language and literacy development of deaf and hard-of-hearing children: successes and challenges. *Developmental psychology*, 49(1):15.

Levy, R. and Andrew, G. (2006). Tregex and Tsurgeon: tools for querying and manipulating tree data structures. In *Proceedings of the Fifth International Conference on Language Resources and Evaluation (LREC).*

Malmsten, M., Börjeson, L., and Haffenden, C. (2020). Playing with words at the national library of Sweden–making a Swedish BERT. *arXiv preprint arXiv:2007.01658.*

Monsen, J. and Jönsson, A. (2021). A method for building non-english corpora for abstractive text summarization. In *Proceedings of CLARIN Annual Conference 2021.*

MTM. (2021). Att skriva lättläst. `https://www.mtm.se/var-verksamhet/lattlast/att-skriva-lattlast/`. Accessed: 2021-10-05.

Mukherjee, P., Leroy, G., Kauchak, D., Rajanarayanan, S., Diaz, D. Y. R., Yuan, N. P., Pritchard, T. G., and

Colina, S. (2017). Negait: A new parser for medical text simplification using morphological, sentential and double negation. *Journal of biomedical informatics*, 69:55–62.

Nilsson, K., Danielsson, H., Elwér, Å., Messer, D., Henry, L., and Samuelsson, S. (2021a). Decoding Abilities in Adolescents with Intellectual Disabilities: The Contribution of Cognition, Language, and Home Literacy. *Journal of Cognition*, 4(1):1–16.

Nilsson, K., Danielsson, H., Elwér, Å., Messer, D., Henry, L., and Samuelsson, S. (2021b). Investigating reading comprehension in adolescents with intellectual disabilites: Evaluating the simple view of reading. *Journal of Cognition*, 4(1):1–16.

Nivre, J., Hall, J., Nilsson, J., Chanev, A., Eryigit, G., Kübler, S., Marinov, S., and Marsi, E. (2007). MaltParser: A language-independent system for data-driven dependency parsing. *Natural Language Engineering*, 13(2):95–135.

Paetzold, G. H. and Specia, L. (2017). A survey on lexical simplification. *Journal of Artificial Intelligence Research*, 60:549–593.

PLAIN. (2011). Federal Plain Language Guidelines.

Rello, L., Baeza-Yates, R., Dempere-Marco, L., and Saggion, H. (2013). Frequent words improve readability and short words improve understandability for people with dyslexia. In *IFIP Conference on Human-Computer Interaction*, pages 203–219. Springer.

Rennes, E. and Jönsson, A. (2015). A tool for automatic simplification of swedish texts. In *Proceedings of the 20th Nordic Conference of Computational Linguistics (NoDaLiDa-2015), Vilnius, Lithuania.*

Rennes, E. and Jönsson, A. (2021). Synonym replacement based on a study of basic-level nouns in swedish texts of different complexity. In *Proceedings of the 23rd Nordic Conference on Computational Linguistics (NoDaLiDa)*, pages 259–267.

Rothe, S., Narayan, S., and Severyn, A. (2020). Leveraging pre-trained checkpoints for sequence generation tasks.

Rybing, J., Smith, C., and Silvervarg, A. (2010). Towards a Rule Based System for Automatic Simplification of Texts. In *Swedish Language Technology Conference, SLTC, Linköping, Sweden.*

Siddharthan, A. (2003). *Syntactic Simplification and Text Cohesion.* Ph.d. thesis, University of Cambridge, UK.

Sjöholm, J. (2012). Probability as readability: A new machine learning approach to readability assessment for written Swedish. Master's thesis, Linköping University.

Smith, C. and Jönsson, A. (2011a). Automatic Summarization As Means Of Simplifying Texts, An Evaluation For Swedish. In *Proceedings of the 18th Nordic Conference of Computational Linguistics (NoDaLiDa-2010), Riga, Latvia.*

Smith, C. and Jönsson, A. (2011b). Enhancing extraction based summarization with outside word space. In *Proceedings of the 5th International Joint Conference on Natural Language Processing, Chiang Mai, Thailand.*

Štajner, S., Popovic, M., and Béchara, H. (2016). Quality estimation for text simplification. In *Proceedings of the LREC Workshop on Quality Assessment for Text Simplification (QATS), Portoroz, Slovenia.*

Vellutino, F. R., Fletcher, J. M., Snowling, M. J., and Scanlon, D. M. (2004). Specific reading disability (dyslexia): What have we learned in the past four decades? *Journal of child psychology and psychiatry*, 45(1):2–40.

Wengelin, Å. (2015). Mot en evidensbaserad språkvård? en kritisk granskning av några svenska klarspråksråd i ljuset av forskning om läsbarhet och språkbearbetning. *Sakprosa*, 7(2).

Östling, R. (2018). Part of speech tagging: Shallow or deep learning? *North European Journal of Language Technology*, 5:1–15.

Proceedings of the 2nd READI Workshop @ LREC2022, pages 39–45
Marseille, 24 June 2022

HIBOU: an eBook to improve Text Comprehension and Reading Fluency for Beginning Readers of French

Ludivine Javourey-Drevet[1,2], Stéphane Dufau[2], Johannes C. Ziegler[2], Núria Gala[3]

[1] Univ Lille, CNRS, SCALab - Sciences Cognitives et Sciences Affectives (UMR 9193)
[2] Aix-Marseille Univ, CNRS, Laboratoire de Psychologie Cognitive (UMR 7290)
[3] Aix-Marseille Univ, CNRS, Laboratoire Parole et Langage (UMR 7309)

ludivine.javourey@univ-lille.fr, {stephane.dufau, johannes.ziegler, nuria.gala}@univ-amu.fr

Abstract

In this paper, we present HIBOU, an eBook application initially developed for iOs, displaying adapted texts (i.e. simplified), and proposing text comprehension activities. The application has been used in six elementary schools in France to evaluate and train reading fluency and comprehension skills on beginning readers of French. HIBOU displays two versions of French literary and documentary texts from the ALECTOR corpus, the 'original', and a simplified version. Text simplifications have been manually performed at the lexical, syntactic, and discursive levels. The child can read in autonomy and has access to different games on word identification. HIBOU is at present being developed to be online in a platform that will be available at elementary schools in France.

Keywords: reading practice, educational device, French L1, text adaptation, text comprehension activities.

1. Introduction

Becoming a fluent reader who easily understands a written text is a major societal issue. Comprehension of a text requires rapid progress from word recognition to the development of a mental representation of the text, based on linguistic analyses and ideas from the text, in connection with knowledge of the world.

1.1 Acquiring reading skills at the early years

Studying the development of children's general reading skills between the ages of 7 and 9 is of outmost importance because it is a decisive phase for the acquisition of automatic word recognition and text comprehension skills. Indeed, it is during this period that children enter the phase of self-teaching (Share, 1995; Ziegler et al., 2014, 2020) and develop automatic reading and text comprehension strategies (Bianco & Lima, 2017; Willingham, 2006). The virtuous circle of self-teaching is initiated when the child starts to use basic spelling-to-sound correspondences to decode novel words. Successful decoding of words (i.e., finding a match in phonological and semantic memory) reinforces the decoding mechanism, and generates an orthographic representation of the word (see Ziegler et al., 2014, 2020 for a computational account of this process). Over time, thanks to repetition, the decoding process becomes more and more efficient, allowing a more rapid transformation of the orthographic to the phonological form of words, thus reducing the cognitive cost of decoding. The child will be able to progressively free cognitive resources for understanding what he or she reads rather than for decoding (Sprenger-Charolles & Ziegler, 2019). Comprehension requires many resources such as language knowledge, cultural knowledge, and cognitive efficiencies (memory, attention, reasoning, executive functions, visual abilities) (Bianco, 2015).

1.2 Reading difficulties

Although most children learn to read during early elementary school, some of them fail to benefit from regular classroom instruction. Some reasons have been put forward in the literature. Vernon-Feagans and collaborators (2010, p. 183) distinguish two groups of struggling readers: "The first group comes to school with adequate oral language skills but has trouble with the processes involved in the relationship between oral language and the printed word. The second, larger group is characterized by problems in both oral language/vocabulary and print related/phonological knowledge. This latter group is composed mostly of low-income children who come to school without the prerequisite experiences in emergent literacy to allow them to profit from most whole class instructional practices".

Failing at the early years of reading instruction creates a gap between struggling readers and their peers, a gap that grows over the years. Three-quarters of students who are poor readers in grade 3 will remain poor readers in high school (Foorman et al., 1997).

In this context, the main contribution of our work is the proposition of an application for beginning readers of French, based on reading practice through simplified versions of literary and documentary texts (see section 4 for more details on text simplification). The tool can be easily used by children during classroom instruction or in autonomy at home (it has already been tested in six French schools from 2017 to 2019, see section 3.1 for details).

The paper is organized as follows. Section 2 reports on research studies related to reading difficulties of beginning readers in France. In the following sections, 3 to 5, we present the eBook HIBOU, the corpus, and the learning activities. To conclude, in section 6 we discuss on developments and evolutions of the eBook.

2. Beginning readers in France: an overview

In France, the CEDRE report (2015) that evaluates if the national educational curriculum at primary school has been achieved, shows that 11 % of children at the end of grade 5 fail to understand a text, i.e. they are unable to extract and analyze explicit and even less implicit information[1].

The international program PIRLS (Progress in International Reading Literacy) suggests that 10 out of 60 countries, in which reading comprehension has been tested with fourth-grade children, show alarmingly low average scores (Mullis et al., 2017). The situation seems particularly problematic in France: 6% of the students (4% in Europe) have a standard score below 400, which is taken as an indicator that they do not master elementary reading and comprehension skills (Mullis et al., 2017). Since the first PIRLS evaluation in 2001, the performance in reading comprehension of French students has dropped year after year, especially for complex reading comprehension skills (e.g., inference) and informative texts (e.g., scientific or documentary texts).

In recent national assessments, in which 4 837 students at grade 2 in France were tested on reading fluency and comprehension (Andreu et al., 2021), it was found that 15.3% had problems in comprehending a text when it was read on their own and 26.9% had difficulties reading aloud. This situation highlights the importance of providing early intervention programs and resources.

One of such intervention programs might be developing reading activities with a resource with simplified texts and playful exercises. As showed by Javourey–Drevet and collaborators (2022), reading training through adapted (i.e. simplified) versions of texts improves fluency and comprehension: children find it easier to get to the meaning of a text, which in turn, might encourage exposure to more written texts. Reading simplified texts helps poor readers and children with weaker cognitive skills (nonverbal intelligence, memory). This solution might also be relevant as a motivational and inclusive strategy in a classroom with all kinds of reader profiles: all children read the same text (in terms of contents), but while regular readers have the original text, struggling readers read an adapted version to achieve the same objectives. The eBook that we present in this paper has been developed to address this issue. In addition to a variety of texts in original or simplified versions, the tool provides several lexical games to allow children to enhance their vocabulary skills.

3. HIBOU: eBook for reading and learning

HIBOU aims at training reading comprehension and fluency.

3.1 Genesis of the project

The project was initiated by the Laboratoire de Psychologie Cognitive (UMR 7290) and the Laboratoire Parole et Langage (UMR 7309) in collaboration with a school district in the South of France (Var) and the regional authority (Communauté d'Agglomération Sud Sainte Baume). HIBOU is an electronic book in Apple format (eBook). This kind of solution was suited for a research project on studying the development of children's general reading skills between the ages of 7 and 9. For several years, we followed the evolution of the reading skills of children in grades 2 to 4.

The research project has now come to an end, but we have decided to make the eBook live beyond the project. We have improved it, we gave it a name, HIBOU, we enriched it with some iconography (see Figure 1) and we made it available for download[2] (right now only for the Apple ecosystem, but an open-access web platform is currently being developed, cf. section 6.2).

Figure 1: HIBOU Logo.

HIBOU has been developed on iPads to initially assess the effects of text simplification in beginning readers of French all profiles combined: regular readers, low-readers, dyslexic readers, etc. Since the eBook has been well received by the teachers, who could use it at different moments in the classrooms, we would like now to enhance the use of HIBOU through an open access web-platform, and to enrich the eBook with more advanced devices (i.e. adaptive learning to consider individual differences and profiles, see section 6.2).

3.2 Assessing the effects of text simplification for improving reading fluency and comprehension

HIBOU has been used in six primary schools in the south of France for three years (2017-2019) to analyze the effects of text simplification in beginning readers of French (Javourey-Drevet, 2021; Javourey-Drevet et al., 2022). It allowed to collect information on reading times during the three years for about 165 children per year. Each participant in each grade (from 2 to 4) read 20 texts (10 literary and 10 documentary, for each category 5 original versions and 5 simplified versions were available). The choice of an adapted version was randomly proposed. After reading a given text, the participant had to answer to a multiple-choice quiz. Besides the reading and comprehension task, ten tests were used to assess the individual cognitive and language profile, proposed in the same order to each participant.

The results of the reading tests showed that text simplification was beneficial for fluency ($F = 81.327$, $P = .000$, $\eta p^2 = .373$) and comprehension ($F = 32.020$, $p = .000$, $\eta p^2 = .189$) over the three years for most students and for both types of texts (Javourey-Drevet, 2021). This suggests that simplification can be effective across the elementary

---

[1] Grade 5 is called '*Cours Moyen*' 2 (CM2) in France.

[2] https://lpc.univ-amu.fr/fr/hibou-livre-interactif

school curriculum. Text simplification does not directly affect text comprehension but rather impacts factors that influence comprehension, such as word recognition, vocabulary, inferences or morphosyntax.
The results of the reading tests for children of grade 2 showed that simplified texts were read faster than original texts (b=-0.03, SD=0.009, t=-3.5), and that scientific texts (b=0.02, SD=0.008, t=2.73) on reaction times were read slower than literary texts. The type of text did not reach significance (t=1.16). We also obtained a significant effect of simplification showing that comprehension was better for simplified texts than for original versions (b=0.55, SD=0.09, z=6.23). The gains in simplification (difference between simplified and original texts) were greater for poor readers than for good readers. For comprehension in scientific documentaries, simplification gains were stronger for children with poor non-verbal intelligence and low working memory (Javourey-Drevet et al., 2022).

4. Corpus and reading settings

The texts available in HIBOU are part of the ALECTOR corpus, a collection of 79 original texts in French with their simplified versions (Gala, 2020a). The corpus is already available online[3] through a platform that proposes different options for visualizing the texts. It also provides the comprehension questions for each text in the form of multiple-choice questions. Most of the texts from ALECTOR (69) have been integrated in HIBOU. On average, the original versions have about 300 words and the adapted versions 275 (both versions are longer in higher levels, going from grade 2 to grade 4). We focused on grades 2 to 4 because the reading programs and activities are part of the curriculum (we left aside grade 1 where children acquire basic decoding skills).
The corpus presents two kind of texts, narrative (literary) and scientific (documentary). While literary texts often reflect the world view and the sensitivity of its author with a language that emphasizes the aesthetics, the rhythm, etc., documentary texts aim at explaining or describing a scientific or technological causality. Scientific texts are descriptive and explanatory with a logical structure based on scientific reasoning. The texts are extracts taken from websites with stories[4] or documentaries[5], selected pieces of magazines (BTJ[6], WAPITI[7] for example), and excerpts of books for children (*Chichois de la rue des Mauvestis*, Ciravégna, 1995, to give an example)[8]. The choice of these genres was motivated by our initial project, keeping in mind that the type of text influences comprehension: narrative texts are more easily understood than informative texts whose topics depend on specific world knowledge (Best et al., 2008; McNamara et al., 2017), see section 4.1.

4.1 Text simplification

Simplifying a text renders word recognition and decoding more efficient for poor readers and children with weaker cognitive abilities, which has direct effects in reading fluency and text comprehension (Javourey-Drevet et al., 2022). Decoding, i.e. linking graphemes and phonemes, must be automated to read words so that he or she can extract the meaning of a sentence and construct an interpretation. Recognizing a written word does not automatically mean comprehending the meaning (Ziegler, Perry & Zorzi, 2014). Comprehension is practiced for both oral and written language. The Simple View of Reading (SVR) model (Gough & Tumner, 1986) describes reading comprehension as the product of word recognition and oral comprehension. Word identification constrains comprehension, but it is also the cognitive component of the comprehension process that determines the successful development of a mental representation from the text.
Language processing requires complex operations in which memory and different processes of control and manipulation of the information are involved. In this context, text simplification can be a temporary aid for pupils with reading difficulties to continue decoding, reading, and enhancing text comprehension. The idea is to reduce the complexity of a text while preserving its original content (Saggion, 2017). By doing this, the text may be more easily read and understood.
Text simplifications in the ALECTOR corpus were manually carried out by a group of researchers in educational sciences, cognitive psychology, linguistics, and speech therapy. It was decided to keep the simplified text as close as possible to the original version to improve readability and understandability while maintaining the original information content. As the corpus was created having in mind the development of a first automatic text simplification system for French (Todirascu at al., 2022), we considered only linguistic transformations that could be later implemented. For instance, we gave priority to lexical substitutions and coreference chains substitutions (providing the referent to a pronoun), and straightforward reformulations (e.g. deletion of subordinate conjunctions to split a long sentence into two, see Gala et al. 2020b). We deliberately avoided reformulations that would have changed the original texts rather drastically (i.e. summarization).
Within the field of Natural Language Processing (NLP), automatic text simplification (ATS) has been explored from different angles since the late 90s, and especially very recently with the rapid growth of statistical and deep learning techniques. However, although being an active research area (see Al-Thanyyan and Azmi (2021) for a complete survey), when we started the project there was not yet a sufficiently satisfactory state-of-the-art tool for automatically simplifying texts in French. Therefore, manual simplifications, although very time-consuming, were the only option to provide adapted reading materials for struggling readers in elementary schools.
The adaptations were made at four linguistic levels: vocabulary and morphology (lexical adaptations), sentence structures (syntactic adaptations) and pronouns (discourse adaptations). Lexical adaptations, i.e. substitutions of words with simpler synonyms (shorter, more frequent, simpler syllable structure, etc.) were performed based on two standard lexical resources for French: Manulex (Lété

[3] https://corpusalector.huma-num.fr/
[4] https://www.storyplayr.com/blog/le-conte-africain
[5] https://kidiscience.cafe-sciences.org/articles/comment-les-huitres-fabriquent-elles-des-perles/
[6] https://www.icem-vente-en-ligne.org/btj
[7] https://www.wapiti-magazine.com/magazine
[8] https://www.babelio.com/livres/Ciravegna-Chichois-de-la-rue-des-Mauvestis/459091

et al., 2004) and ReSyf[9] (Billami et al., 2018). Syntactic and discursive simplifications followed a set of guidelines that we defined to address the specificities of poor and dyslexic children's needs (Gala et al., 2020b; Wilkens & Todirascu, 2020). The guidelines include a total of 29 recommendations: six for typography (e.g., police size, interlinear and character spacing, etc.), five for lexical substitutions (thus characterizing simpler synonym candidates), five for morphology (e.g. frequencies in morphological families, verb-tenses, etc.), nine for syntax (e.g. keeping the SVO order when possible, split complex sentences, avoid negation, etc.), and five for discourse related difficulties (e.g., pronoun substitution with a referent, replacement of certain determinants, etc.). The guidelines are free available on-line in the web-site of the ALECTOR project[10].

The simplification effort was different according to the type of text. The specific vocabulary of documentary texts, often unknown to young readers, was difficult to adapt because of its specialization (Marin et al., 2007). In these cases, we preferred to keep the original word (e.g., although being words with a complex structure -graphemes, complex syllables, etc.- we kept "atmosphere" and "scaphandre", respectively *'atmosphere'* and *'diving suit',* instead of trying to provide semantic equivalents). In literary texts, vocabulary adaptations were easier to perform thanks to synonymy (e.g. "mousquetaire" replaced by "soldat", *'musketeer'* by *'soldier'*). We choose the closest semantic synonym, knowing that full synonymy is rare, and unstable where it does exist (Murphy, 2003, p. 165).

4.2 Reading settings in the eBook

HIBOU displays ten different pages. The first one contains a web application integrated into the book, the other pages display pedagogical information and the first sentences of the texts to be read. The heart of HIBOU is the web application.

The reader can choose a text depending on his/her level at primary school (beginner = grade 2, intermediate = grade 3, advanced = grades 4 and 5). The complexity of the texts increases according to the level (longer texts, more complex structures, and more specialized vocabulary). There is currently an average of 20 texts per level.

The texts are presented sentence by sentence (it has been shown that presenting texts line by line on electronic devices can improve reading speed and comprehension for struggling readers (Schneps et al., 2013)). The reader can also set up between-character and between-line spacing (Zorzi et al., 2012). The spacing of letters and words allows learners to be less influenced by the presence of neighboring letters and words when reading a word (i.e., crowding).

After choosing the level of a text, from "Beginner" to "Advanced", the child (or the teacher) chooses among the category "*Défi*" for texts in the simplified version or "*Challenge*" for texts in the original version. On the page displaying the texts, an icon corresponds to the theme of the text (see Figure 2). A different color indicates the type of text: green frame for literary texts and red for documentaries.

[9] https://cental.uclouvain.be/resyf/

The application was designed to allow researchers to collect reading times from the readers. By using these data, it was possible to implement an alert message (*"you read too fast!"*, see Figure 3) when the reading time was below the minimum threshold according to the number of words in the sentence.

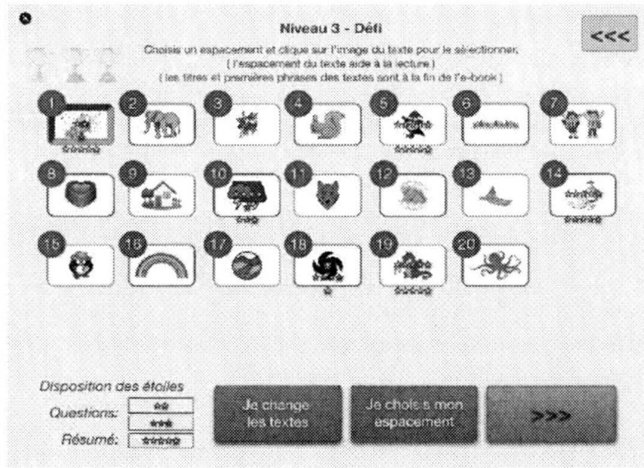

Figure 2: HIBOU interface for choosing the texts.

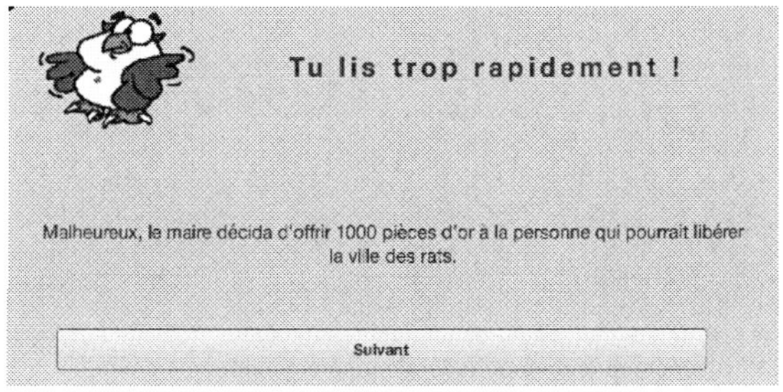

Figure 3: HIBOU interface for reading sentence after sentence, and error message.

5. Learning activities

In addition to the reading activities, using HIBOU the child can improve his/her comprehension of the texts and work on his/her vocabulary through different word-games.

5.1 Multiple choice questions

After reading a text, a **multiple-choice questionnaire** is presented: five questions are asked to the child and for each of them three or four possible answers are proposed. The five questions are based on essential elements or events that are present within the whole text. They are displayed following the chronological order in which they appear in the text. The questions allow the child to consider the overall understanding of the text, sometimes by doing inferences. The proposed answers to each question are all plausible and related to the subject of the text.

For levels 2 and 3, a **gap-fill summary** is also provided (see Figure 4). Five words must be put in the right place in the text. For each text, we proposed the same grammatical category for statements, e.g. only nouns or only verbs. We also balanced the different grammatical categories between literary and scientific texts.

[10] https://alectorsite.files.wordpress.com/2020/11/guidelines-linguistiques_alector_final.pdf

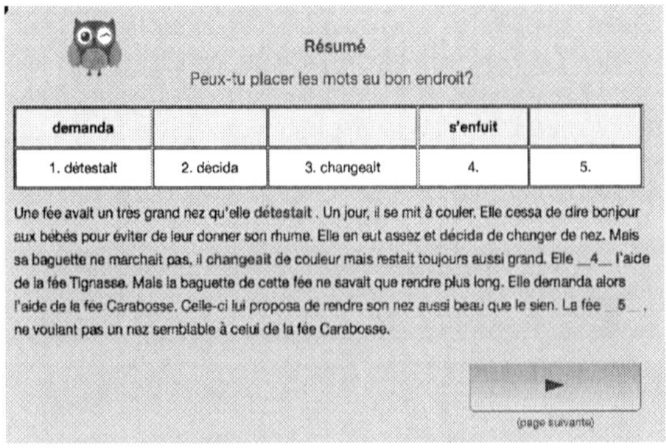

Figure 4: HIBOU interface for gap-fill summary.

The comprehension activity has been imagined as a game enabling to get awards. Correct answers to the quiz and the gap-fill summary give the child gold or silver stars which are displayed on the text selection page. Golden stars are proposed for correct answers; silver stars for inaccurate answers (one or more elements are present in the text). If the answer is totally incorrect, no reward is offered. For the gap-fill summary activity, each word or group of words correctly positioned provides a gold star (see Figure 5).

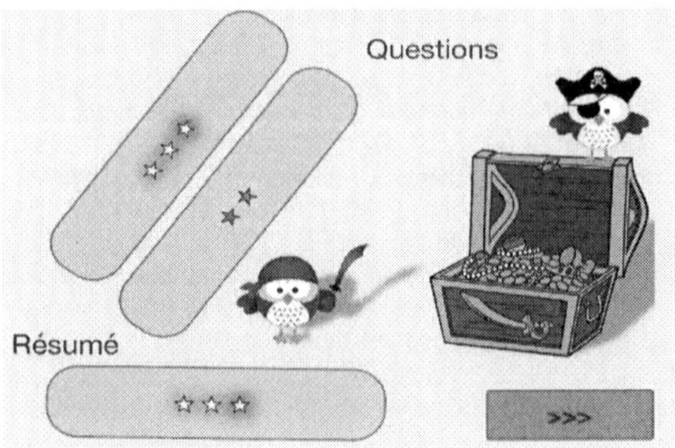

Figure 5: HIBOU interface for individual rewards after reading a text.

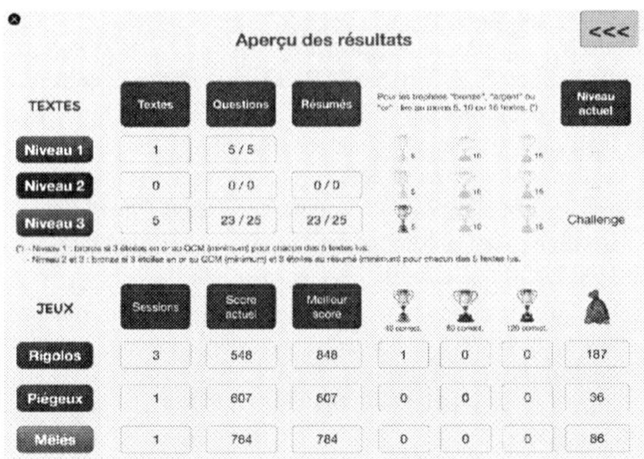

Figure 6: HIBOU interface for overall rewards.

Children can read a text several times before doing the questionnaire. They can also redo the assessment if they are not satisfied with their performance, but only after rereading the text.

Finally, a page allows the child to quickly see the number of texts already read, the score obtained in the questions and summaries (see Figure 6). The number of activities allows the child to win a cup: bronze trophy for 5 texts read, silver trophy for 10 texts read and gold trophy for 15 texts read.

5.2 Word identification

HIBOU proposes three word-games, two on spelling recognition and one focused on syntax and semantics. The games are based on a choice task between two alternatives, which is called lexical decision. The player chooses whether the word or sequence of words, presented in the center of the screen, is correct or not. A sound feedback allows the child to know whether his or her answer is right or wrong, so that he or she only memorizes a correct spelling.

The first word game, *Mots Rigolos* (Funny Words), is intended for readers of all levels. It is based on words from textbooks. The nonwords are constructed so that they do not look like words, for example “pamelut”, “mias”, “placiter”, “nediter”, etc.

The second word game, *Pièges piégeux* (Trapping Traps), is intended for good readers. The traps are constructed mainly by changing the spelling of words, for example “exemqle”, “brôle” (“drôle” *funny*), “ensemfle” (“ensemble” *together*), “doucemen” (“doucement” *slowly*).

The third word game, *Mots Mêlés* (Mixed Words), is a game on sentences or phrases. Here, the trap sequences are utterances where the words have been scrambled (the SVO or syntagmatic order is not maintained). These utterances do not make sense and are not grammatically or syntactically correct, for instance “inquiets se très montrent” for “se montrent très inquiets” (*they are very worried*), “dresse sur il se” for “il se dresse sur” (*he stands upright*), “pas ne copie on” for “on ne copie pas” (*do not copy*), “bateau de son l'arrière” for “l'arrière de son bateau” (*the back of his boat*). The child must reorder the sequence. The players earn coins if they answer quickly and correctly. An overall score is also given at the end of each game, along with a reading speed in words per minute. The score can be improved by playing several times.

6. Implementation and future work

6.1 From iPads to an online application

As previously mentioned, the heart of the eBook is the interactive embedded web application: the reading application is programmed in HTML5 with some API such as Canvas and Web Storage, user interface and interactions are managed by Javascript routines and content of texts, questions and answers are stored in JSON format. HIBOU application can run on all versions of the iPad family, although sounds do not play correctly on iPad2 and earlier versions.

Originally developed as an eBook (Apple standard), the technical specifications of the iPad application make it suitable to be transferred to similar environments such as computers and tablets displaying a standard e-book (EPUB3 international standard). Such a development has recently been carried out by an industrial partner of the original HIBOU project (ISI Inc., France) that publishes electronic books for schools. The new e-book will be available by the end of 2022 with a tier policy that will make the access to the content free of charge for pupils.

6.2 Future work

Right now HIBOU has been used in six French schools and all the readers performances in the period 2017-2019 have been logged. There is currently work in progress on the analysis on the performances on the different kind of texts (literary *vs* documentary, original *vs* simplified) on the tested school levels (2-4).
In future work, we plan to enrich the corpus with more literary and documentary texts, along with their comprehension tasks, particularly for grade 5. As a result, the platform will provide texts addressed to children of all primary levels (grade 2 to 5). While in the long run, part of the simplifications will become semi-automatized by using a text simplification system for French (work in progress), in the short-term, we will train a group of teachers on text simplification to be able to increase the corpus and the associated learning activities.
Finally, we are planning the possibility to include adaptive learning devices thanks to IA, to propose specific texts and vocabulary activities adapted to each individual profile. By collecting individual feedback on how the child browses the texts and activities, the platform will be able to guide the learners by proposing them adapted materials. By doing so, HIBOU will enable weaker readers to progress at their rhythm while reading the same texts than normal readers. It will be able to propose new adapted tasks for training, thus encouraging them to read more.

7. Conclusion

Adapting texts to the needs of struggling readers might be a solution to enhance reading practices and to boost reading comprehension. In this paper, we have proposed HIBOU, and eBook enabling to read and play with words to enhance reading practices and vocabulary skills. While it has been initially developed in the Apple ecosystem, we are now preparing an open access platform that will be freely available to teachers and learners of French.
In future work, we plan to enrich HIBOU with more texts by recruiting and training teachers on text simplification. We are also interested in applying recent advances in automatic text simplification in French to assist the teachers in the work of adapting the texts. Finally, we are foreseeing the possibility to include adaptive learning devices thanks to AI, to propose specific texts and vocabulary activities adapted to each individual profile.

8. Acknowledgements

This work has been supported by the pilot center on teacher training and research for education (AMPIRIC), funded by the Future Investment Program (PIA3), and the center of excellence on Language, Communication and Brain (ILCB), funded by the French National Agency for Research (ANR, ANR-16-CONV-0002) and the Excellence Initiative of Aix-Marseille University A*MIDEX (ANR-11-IDEX-0001-02). The research was directly funded through grants from the ANR, ALECTOR (ANR-16-CE28-0005) and MORPHEME (ANR-15-FRAL-0003-01) and the ERC (Advanced grant 742141). The authors thank all the participants, the teachers who accepted to use the eBooks in their classrooms, and the school authorities who supported this study, especially Olivier Millangue, Nathalie Greppo-Chaignon, and Géraldine Gaudino. We also thank the Communauté d'Agglomération Sud Sainte Baume for providing access to the iPads used in the schools and for their technical support.

9. Bibliographical References

Al-Thanyyan, S. and Azmi, A. (2021) Automated Text Simplification: A Survey. *ACM Computing Surveys* 54(2), article n° 43, 36 pages.

Andreu, S., Cioldi, I., Conceicao, P., Desclau, J., Eteve, Y., Fabre, M., Laskowski, C., Le Breton, S., Neirac, L., Persem, E., Portelli, T., Rocher, T., Rue, G., Thumerelle, J., Vourc'h, R. & Wuillamier, P. (2021). « Evaluations 2021 Repères CP, CE1 : premiers résultats » série études, n°21-E06, novembre 2021, DEPP.

Best, R., Floyd, R. G., & Mcnamara, D. S. (2008). Differential competencies contributing to children's comprehension of narrative and expository texts. *Reading psychology*, 29(2), 137-164.

Bianco, M. (2015). *Du langage oral à la compréhension de l'écrit.* PUG.

Bianco, M., & Lima, L. (2017). *Comment enseigner la compréhension en lecture ?* Hatier.

Billami, M., François, T. & Gala, N. (2018) ReSyf: a French lexicon with ranked synonyms. In *Proceedings of the 27th International Conference on Computational Linguistics* (COLING 2018), Santa Fe, US, 2570-2581.

Foorman, B. R., Francis, D. J., Shaywitz, S. E., Shaywitz, B. A., & Fletcher, J. M. (1997). The case for early reading intervention. In B. A. Blachman (Ed.), *Foundations of reading acquisition and dyslexia: Implications for early intervention*, 243–264. Lawrence Erlbaum Associates Publishers.

Gala, N., Tack, A., Javourey-Drevet, L., François, T., & Ziegler, J. C. (2020a, May). Alector: A parallel corpus of simplified French texts with alignments of misreadings by poor and dyslexic readers. In *Language Resources and Evaluation for Language Technologies (LREC)*. European Language Resources Association, Marseille, France, 1353-1361.

Gala, N., Todirascu, A., Javourey-Drevet, L., Bernhard, L. & Wilkens, R. (2020b). Recommandations pour des transformations de textes français afin d'améliorer leur lisibilité et leur compréhension. [Guidelines for transforming French texts to improve their readability and comprehension] Report prepared for Agence Nationale de la Recherche (ANR), ALECTOR (ANR-16-CE28-0005), Paris, France.

Gough, P. B., & Tunmer, W. E. (1986). Decoding, reading, and reading disability. *Remedial and special education*, 7(1), 6-10. https://doi.org/10.1177/074193258600700104

Javourey-Drevet, L. (2021). *La simplification de textes comme outil pour améliorer la fluidité et la compréhension de lecture chez les enfants à l'école primaire: une étude en longitudinal avec des textes littéraires et scientifiques chez des enfants entre 7 et 9 ans*. PhD doctoral dissertation, Aix-Marseille Université.

Javourey-Drevet, L., Dufau, S., François, T., Gala, N., Ginestié, J., & Ziegler, J. (2022). Simplification of literary and scientific texts to improve reading fluency and comprehension in beginning readers of French. *Applied Psycholinguistics, 43*(2), 485-512. doi:10.1017/S014271642100062X

Lété, B., Sprenger-Charolles, L., & Colé, P. (2004). MANULEX: A grade-level lexical database from French elementary school readers. *Behavior Research Methods*, Instruments, & Computers, 36(1), 156–166.

Marin, B., Crinon, J., Legros, D., & Avel, P. (2007). Lire un texte documentaire scientifique : quels obstacles, quelles aides à la compréhension ? *Revue française de pédagogie. Recherches en éducation,* (160), 119-131.

McNamara, D. S., Ozuru, Y., & Floyd, R. G. (2017). Comprehension challenges in the fourth grade: The roles of text cohesion, text genre, and readers' prior knowledge. International electronic journal of elementary education, 4(1), 229-257.

Mullis, I. V. S., Martin, M. O., Foy, P., & Hooper, M. (2017). PIRLS 2016 International Results in Reading. Retrieved from Boston College, TIMSS & PIRLS International Study Center website.

Murphy, M. L. (2003) *Semantic relations and the lexicon: Antonymy, synonymy and other paradigms*. Cambridge University Press.

Saggion, H. (2017). *Automatic Text Simplification. Synthesis Lectures on Human Language Technologies*, Califormia, Morgan & Claypool Publishers.

Schneps, M. H., Thomson, J. M., Chen, C., Sonnert, G., & Pomplun, M. (2013). E-Readers Are More Effective than Paper for Some with Dyslexia. *PLoS ONE*, 8(9), e75634. doi: 10.1371/journal.pone.0075634

Share, D. L. (1995). Phonological recoding and self-teaching: Sine qua non of reading acquisition. *Cognition*, 55(2), 151-218.

Sprenger-Charolles, L., & Ziegler, J. C. (2019). Apprendre à lire : contrôle, automatismes et auto-apprentissage. Dans Bentolila, A & Germain, B (dir.), *L'apprentissage de la lecture*, 95-109, Nathan.

Todirascu, A., Wilkens, R., Rolin, E., François, T., Bernhard, D. & Gala, N. (2022) HECTOR: a Hybrid Text Simplification Tool for Raw Texts in French. In *proceedings of 13th International conference on Language Resources and Evaluation (LREC 2022),* Marseille, France.

Vernon-Feagans, L., Gallagher, K., Ginsberg, M.-C., Amendum, S., Kainz, K., Rose, J. & Burchinal, M. (2010). A Diagnostic Teaching Intervention for Classroom Teachers: Helping Struggling Readers in Early Elementary School. In *Learning Disabilities Research & Practice*, 25(4), 183-193.

Wilkens, R. & Todirascu, A. (2020). Simplifying Coreference Chains for Dyslexic Children. Proceedings of the 12th *International conference on Language Resources and Evaluation* for Language Technologies (LREC 2020), Marseille, France.

Willingham, D. T. (2006). The usefulness of brief instruction in reading comprehension strategies. American Educator, 30(4), 39-50.

Ziegler, J. C., Perry, C., & Zorzi, M. (2014). Modelling reading development through phonological decoding and self-teaching: Implications for dyslexia. Philosophical *Transactions of the Royal Society B: Biological Sciences*, 369(1634), 20120397.

Ziegler, J. C., Perry, C., & Zorzi, M. (2020). Learning to Read and Dyslexia: From Theory to Intervention Through Personalized Computational Models. *Current Directions in Psychological Science*, 0963721420915873.

Zorzi, M., Barbiero, C., Facoetti, A., Lonciari, I., Carrozzi, M., Montico, M., Bravar, L., George, F., Pech-Georgel, C., & Ziegler, J. C. (2012). Extra-large letter spacing improves reading in dyslexia. Proceedings of the *National Academy of Sciences*, 109(28), 11455-11459.

Proceedings of the 2nd READI Workshop @ LREC2022, pages 46–53
Marseille, 24 June 2022

PADDLe: a Platform to Identify Complex Words for Learners of French as a Foreign Language (FFL)

Camille Pirali[1], Thomas François[1,2], Núria Gala[3]
[1]Université catholique de Louvain, Belgium [2]CENTAL, IL&C
[3]Aix-Marseille Univ., CNRS, Laboratoire Parole et Langage (UMR 7309), France
camille.pirali@student.uclouvain.be, thomas.francois@uclouvain.be, nuria.gala@univ-amu.fr

Abstract

Annotations of word difficulty by readers provide invaluable insights into lexical complexity. Yet, there is currently a paucity of tools allowing researchers to gather such annotations in an adaptable and simple manner. This article presents PADDLe, an online platform aiming to fill that gap and designed to encourage best practices when collecting difficulty judgements. Studies crafted using the tool ask users to provide a selection of demographic information, then to annotate a certain number of texts and answer multiple-choice comprehension questions after each text. Researchers are encouraged to use a multi-level annotation scheme, to avoid the drawbacks of binary complexity annotations. Once a study is launched, its results are summarised in a visual representation accessible both to researchers and teachers, and can be downloaded in .csv format. Some findings of a pilot study designed with the tool are also provided in the article, to give an idea of the types of research questions it allows to answer.

Keywords: Text Simplification, Complex Word Identification, Lexical Difficulty, Lexical Complexity Prediction, Annotation Tool

1. Introduction

The importance of reading for language development, whether in an L1 or an L2, has been argued many times. However, in order for incidental learning of new vocabulary through reading to take place, it is necessary for the reader to already be familiar with the majority of the words they encounter (Huckin and Coady, 1999; Coady, 1996). Presenting readers with texts of an adequate difficulty level is thus essential to foster their reading skills and vocabulary development. This can be achieved either by comparing reading materials and choosing one of the desired level, or by simplifying elements of a text that are too complex. Both cases require to identify potential sources of difficulty for readers, notably on the lexical level.

Predicting how difficult a word will be for a reader requires large amounts of data, which should ideally be collected directly from the target population. Italian-speaking learners of French, for instance, are likely to struggle with different aspects of the language than Japanese speakers, who in turn will not have the same needs as French-speaking readers with dyslexia. Despite this fact, most of the literature devoted to predicting lexical complexity on the basis of difficulty annotations disregards demographic information and produces reader-independent measures of complexity. This one-size-fits-all approach is a first issue that we wish to address in this article.

A second issue is that there is a lack of tools and resources to collect such annotations of lexical difficulty. Indeed, researchers are typically faced with two options: they can either use crowdsourcing websites and create a batch of Human Intelligence Tasks (HITs) to be completed by workers, or create a custom-made platform from scratch. Both of these approaches present shortcomings that can be prohibitive: the first option tends to be expensive and may impose unwanted constraints on the format of the study, while the second requires web programming knowledge and can be very time-consuming. This is a shame, as it may render such studies inaccessible for some, despite them providing valuable insights for the scientific community.

The tool presented in this paper aims to make the process of collecting annotations simpler and accessible for other languages than English, as well as to encourage researchers to collect and account for demographic data. Designed primarily in order to analyse lexical difficulty for learners of French as a foreign language (FFL), it could easily be adapted to different target groups as well. Moreover, the tool strives to involve foreign language teachers in the data collection process, by allowing them to view their students' answers in real time and gain insights into the needs of their class.

The following section (2) will give an overview of previous methodologies employed when collecting similar data, in order to define key features that need to be taken into account. Section 3 will then describe the online platform PADDLe, highlighting the ways it responds to those observations and giving a few pointers on possible use cases. In Section 4, some results from a pilot study conducted through the platform will be presented. Finally, concluding remarks and some future areas of improvement will be proposed in Section 5.

2. Related Work

The task of identifying words which might pose a problem to readers has been referred to as Complex Word Identification (CWI) or Lexical Complexity Prediction

(LCP), depending on whether complexity is conceptualised on a binary or on a continuous scale.

2.1. Complexity Annotation Datasets

The success of a model attempting to predict lexical complexity is impacted by its architecture and the relevance of the selected features, but also by the quality of the data with which it is trained. This was made evident during the 2016 SemEval workshop (Paetzold and Specia, 2016), when the shortcomings of the dataset provided to participating teams for the CWI shared task were such that all teams performed rather poorly (Shardlow et al., 2021b).

The dataset collected for the shared task contained sentences extracted from corpora based on the standard and simplified versions of Wikipedia. Those sentences were annotated by non-native speakers of English, who were asked to assign a binary complexity label to each lexical word of a given sentence. A value of 1 indicated that the annotator could not understand the target word, regardless of whether they understood the meaning of the sentence as a whole. Sentences destined to make up the training set were annotated by 20 people each, while those forming the test set only received one annotation. Furthermore, the corpus was split in a rather unconventional way, with the test set being over forty times larger than the training set (Paetzold and Specia, 2016). This contributed to the complexity of the task according to Shardlow et al. (2021b), and is probably largely responsible for the poor results obtained by the submitted systems.

To build their predictive models, participating teams were presented with two versions of the training set. One version provided all individual annotations for each word, and was used by some teams to fine-tune their model. The other attributed a single tag to each word based on whether at least one reader had found it difficult (Paetzold and Specia, 2016). As a result, a word being marked as complex by only one of the annotators was considered just as complex as another to which all 20 annotators attributed a score of 1. Moreover, as pointed out by Shardlow et al. (2021b), binary complexity judgements rely on an arbitrary threshold decided upon by each annotator. A value of 1 in the training set might therefore have represented very different levels of complexity, which added to the overall difficulty of the challenge.

The subsequent edition of the task, organised in 2018, refined the collection and presentation of the data, which seems to have had a positive impact on the performance of submitted systems (Yimam et al., 2018). The second CWI shared task made use of a multilingual corpus, with languages being represented either in both the training and the test set (English, German, Spanish), or only in the test set (French). Annotations were collected through crowdsourcing, using Amazon Mechanical Turk (MTurk). This time, the data were split so that there would be a larger amount of training sentences than test sentences, and words in the test set received several annotations. Complexity was once again represented as a binary value, with a threshold of only one annotation required for a word to be considered complex. Interestingly, however, participants also received probabilistic values based on the proportion of annotators who did not understand a given word (Yimam et al., 2018). Unfortunately, such a probabilistic annotation system was not enough to make up for the shortcomings of binary annotations, as suggested by Shardlow et al. (2021b), who observed that a value of 0.5 only meant that a word was found complex by half of the annotators - and thus simple by the other half. As such, no direct conclusions could be drawn about its level of complexity.

The organisers of the shared task made several other methodological decisions that differed from the previous edition. While in 2016 the words to be annotated were predefined and presented in a sentence, this time annotators were given a paragraph of five to ten lines in which they were free to select up to ten complex items. This constraint might have had an impact on how complete the data were: indeed, it is possible that annotators sometimes had to make a choice when they had identified more than ten words they thought were complex. A second difference with the first edition of the task was that annotators were asked to identify complex multi-word expressions (MWEs) as well as complex words. This, combined with the fact that words were not preselected, might have impacted the data negatively as well. Indeed, Gooding and Kochmar (2018) reported that certain sequences of words were interpreted as single words by some of the annotators, and as MWEs by others. As for the annotators themselves, they were no longer non-native speakers selecting complex words based on their own understanding of them, but a mix of natives and non-natives who were asked to identify items that could be difficult for learners or people with a reading impairment (Yimam et al., 2018). This is an important distinction to make, as it is likely that some annotators selected words that they themselves understood, but assumed other people might not. The predictions obtained from those annotations might therefore not be equally reliable for all target profiles, and perhaps especially so for readers with a learning or reading disability.

Based on the limitations of those two shared tasks, Shardlow et al. (2021b) formulated a list of guidelines for future CWI datasets. These guidelines are:

1. The annotations should be continuous rather than binary;
2. The items to be annotated should be presented in context;
3. Multiple instances of a same item should be included in the dataset;
4. Each item should receive several annotations;

5. Annotators should represent a variety of profiles in terms of fluency and background;
6. Texts included in the corpus should represent different genres;
7. Both single words and multi-word expressions should be considered in the annotation process.

2.2. Recent Refinements

It is with these recommendations in mind that Shardlow et al. (2021a) compiled their own dataset for the 2021 shared task on Lexical Complexity Prediction. Similarly to Yimam et al. (2018), they collected annotations through crowdsourcing, using the Figure Eight (previously Crowdflower, now Appen) and Amazon Mechanical Turk platforms. They asked annotators to label the complexity of a word using a 5-point Likert scale, and took the mean of all annotations for an item as its gold-standard complexity. This system allowed them to obtain continuous values ranging from 0 to 1, thus moving from a binary classification task (complex or not complex) towards a prediction task estimating how complex a given word is. The items to annotate were preselected and presented in context, and each token occurred at least twice. Teams were therefore encouraged to take context into account when predicting complexity. Finally, the texts used to produce the dataset were taken from three diverse genres, and multi-word expressions were considered alongside single words in the annotation process.

Systems submitted for the task obtained encouraging results, with the highest-ranking teams being very close together in score. This implies that different approaches succeeded in modelling the data almost equally well, which can be interpreted as being a testament to the dataset's quality just as much as to the ingenuity of the participating teams. The recommendations laid out by Shardlow et al. (2021b) thus seem to be genuinely helpful when compiling a dataset for Lexical Complexity Prediction. It is why the tool presented in this paper was devised in a way that would allow researchers to adhere to each of the guidelines when gathering lexical difficulty annotation data.

A fundamental specificity of the three tasks presented above is that they aim to obtain a singular complexity value (whether binary or continuous), conceptualised as being intrinsic to the word itself and not dependent on the reader. What this means is that they assume a word to be somewhat universally complex or non-complex because of the characteristics it possesses, such as its frequency or its length. Inter-rater variability is expected, but seen almost as "noise" in the data resulting from subjective judgements rather than as a phenomenon of interest in itself. By contrast, when building a Text Simplification tool with a specific public in mind, the focus is likely to benefit from being shifted to lexical difficulty (*i.e.* how difficult someone perceives a word to be, based on their particular language knowledge) instead of complexity. Indeed, people are likely to have different simplification needs based on characteristics such as their proficiency level, reading disability or mother tongue. As a result, trying to predict their needs from those of a heterogeneous group might not always yield satisfactory results.

This idea is confirmed by the very low mean inter-rater agreement obtained in the 2016 edition of the CWI task (Krippendorff's α of 0.244) (Paetzold and Specia, 2016). Similarly, Yimam et al. (2017) reported lower agreement scores between non-native speakers than between native speakers of English, most likely due to the fact that the first group is more diverse in terms of language background and proficiency level. Agreement between the two groups was also low, which according to the authors indicates that their simplification needs might differ. As for the third edition of the task, (Shardlow et al., 2021a) didn't report any inter-rater agreement scores.

Since the three tasks did not aim to predict complexity for different groups of readers, no demographic data were provided to the participating teams, even though they had been collected for the first two editions. Nevertheless, Paetzold and Specia (2016) observed that the number of words deemed complex by an annotator was correlated with their age as well as level of proficiency in English. This goes to show that, as suggested by Gooding and Kochmar (2018), including demographic information at both the annotation and the prediction steps should increase the performance of models.

In a study whose methodology was inspired by the shared tasks, Tack (2021) addressed their shortcoming by taking individual differences into account. Via a custom-made online reading interface, L2 learners of French were presented with a set of texts (as opposed to sentences or paragraphs) based on their fluency level, so that all readers of the same level would annotate the same texts. They were asked to highlight any word that they personally found difficult, hence providing annotations of a binary nature. Two trials were organised to gather data: one with a smaller pool of participants (n = 9) with diverse L1 backgrounds, and one with a much bigger pool of participants (n = 47) all sharing the same mother tongue. An inter-rater analysis carried out for all annotators in the first trial yielded very similar results to those of Paetzold and Specia (2016), with a Krippendorff's α of 0.26. Grouping the annotators by proficiency level did not seem to have a clear impact on the metric: A2 readers got an α of 0.23, and B1 readers one of 0.30. Interestingly, the agreement rate between participants in the second trial, once grouped by proficiency level, was much higher: between 0.36 (B1 level) and 0.51 (B2 level). These results suggest that annotators with a similar profile (same mother tongue, proficiency level, education level and age, in this case) tend to agree more in their difficulty judgements than annotators with diverse profiles, which confirms the value of including demographic information in a CWI dataset.

It also follows that reading aids targeting a specific profile, such as dyslexic readers, adults with low literacy or L2 learners with a specific L1, would be likely to benefit from gathering data directly from that target population.

2.3. Summary and goals of our study

This brief overview of previous approaches to CWI/LCP dataset collection has shown the process to be a complex one, requiring many methodological decisions to be made. As the quality of the dataset appears to have a strong impact on the performance of models trained on it, making the right choices is of critical importance. This is why we created a tool that makes it possible for users to almost effortlessly design their own data collection process, and that encourages them to follow the recommendations formulated above. This tool will be further described in the next section.

3. Presentation of the Tool

PADDLe (Plateforme d'Annotation De la Difficulté LExicale) is an online platform[1] hosted by CENTAL, whose aim is to make CWI data collection easier. It currently only supports French, but should include a variety of other languages in the future. It allows researchers to create highly customisable web-based reading tasks and download the data in an easily parsable .csv format.
The tool sets out to make following the guidelines proposed by Shardlow et al. (2021b) easy. Researchers are encouraged to define a continuous annotation scale and to include multi-word expressions, as well as to gather demographic information from participants (which would make them aware of how diverse their annotator pool is). The platform plans for words to be presented in context, and for several participants to annotate the same texts. Finally, researchers are free to add as many texts as they want, and can thus easily include several instances of a word as well as texts of various genres in their corpus.

3.1. Interest

PADDLe was conceived to offer an alternative to other online survey builders. It is completely free of use, customisable, designed specifically for CWI data collection and does not require any web development knowledge. It also allows teachers who ask their students to participate in a reading task to view the results of their class afterwards, to thank them for their contribution.

3.2. Functionalities and Options

The design decisions made when developing PADDLe were based on the conclusions drawn from the literature presented in section 2. The reading tasks created through the platform have the following format:

1. **Demographic form**: Participants answer a series of questions selected by the researchers;
2. **Text annotation**: Participants annotate a text by clicking on words and MWEs they find difficult, according to an annotation scale. The scale, as well as the boundaries of clickable units, are defined by the researchers.
3. **Reading comprehension questions**: Participants' global comprehension of the text is tested using multiple choice questions. Once they submit their answers, participants are given feedback on whether they answered correctly.

Step 2 and 3 are repeated as many times as decided by the researcher before the study ends. All three steps of the task can be customised as follows:

1. **Demographic form**: Researchers can select any of the following: participants' identifier (if they don't want the data to be anonymous), age, country of origin, education level, target language proficiency level, other languages known and proficiency level in each of those languages, time spent learning the target language in a non-native context / in a native context, learning or readings disabilities, and "other" (which gives them the option to add an open question).
2. **Text annotation**: The task can include as many texts as necessary, and researchers can decide whether annotators will read all texts or only a subset of them. In the second case, participants can be presented with a) a set of texts chosen at random, b) all texts of a pre-defined and randomly selected group or c) one text drawn at random from each predetermined group. For each text, researchers provide a title, the id to use in the .csv files and the text itself, which must be formatted as one word or punctuation sign by line. This allows multi-word expressions (or other groups of words that are to be annotated as a unit) to be defined, by simply grouping them on the same line. Punctuation is not made clickable for annotators.
Researchers are also asked to provide an annotation scheme to be used in the reading task: each annotation level is given a colour and a label. Currently, the interface only allows to have between 2 and 5 levels (in addition to the "no annotation" level). This is to encourage users to choose a non-binary scale of annotation.
3. **Reading comprehension questions**: For each text, users are asked to provide between 1 and 6 comprehension questions, each with 2 to 5 possible answers. They must also indicate which of the answers is correct.

Other parts of the study are customisable as well, such as the consent form to be read by participants before beginning the task or the text presenting the study on its home page.

[1]It is available at this address.

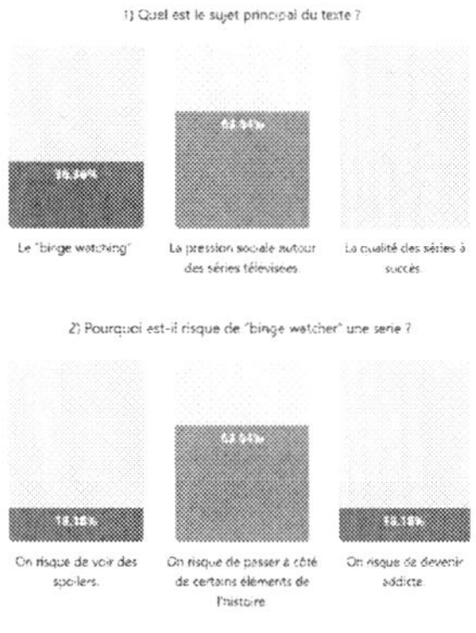

Figure 1: Visual representation of participants' answers to the comprehension questions.

3.3. Possible Uses

All the options presented above aim to make the generated studies as malleable as possible. Instead of whole texts, users of the platform could decide to only include paragraphs, or even sentences. Similarly, they could decide to ask for annotations at the phrase or at the sentence level, by grouping words in a way that suits their research purposes.
As a result, PADDLe could be used to answer a variety of research questions. One could for instance investigate the link between the proportion of words perceived as difficult and the quality of the general comprehension, based on the questions asked after each text. It could also serve to rate different simplifications of a text, in order to find the one readers understand best, or to compare a system's lexical complexity predictions with empirical difficulty judgements.
Outside of academic research, it could also prove an interesting tool for teachers who would like to pinpoint their students' difficulties. By asking all members of a class to annotate the same text and answer a few questions at the end, teachers could then refer to the visual representation of the results provided by the platform to immediately identify the words or aspects of the text found most difficult by the group. Figure 1 provides an example of said representation.

4. Pilot Study

To test the proper functioning and scientific interest of the interface before it could be used for larger research projects, a preliminary study was carried out in November 2021 with a small group of 16 L2 learners of French. It yielded some interesting first results, a selection of which will be presented in what follows.
The group was vastly homogeneous, as participants were all 18 year old students from Malaysia who shared the same mother tongue, all belonged to the B1 level in French and were currently following French classes at the Service Universitaire de Langues (SUL, Aix-Marseille university, France). The study used a total of three informative texts, and each participant was asked to annotate two of them - one seen by all participants (B1 level), and one randomly drawn from the remaining two texts (B2 level). As a result, the number of annotations is not balanced between the texts. Participants were asked to answer five comprehension questions after each text, in order to test their global understanding.

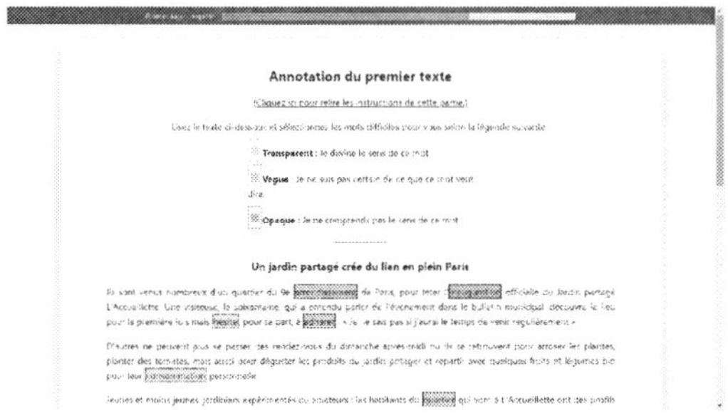

Figure 2: Example of annotation.

The annotation scale employed in the study, inspired by the Vocabulary Knowledge Scale (Wesche and Paribakht, 1996), a revised version of it (Sugiyama, 2017) and the scale used in the 2021 LCP task (Shardlow et al., 2021b), was the following:

0. **Easy** word, no annotation;
1. **Transparent** word (Unknown, but can guess the meaning in context);
2. **Vague** word (Unsure of the meaning);
3. **Opaque** word (Cannot understand the word at all).

Each difficulty level was represented by a colour and outline, indicated in a legend above the text. All words started on 0, and participants could click on a word to cyclically increase its difficulty level (once for "transparent", twice for "vague", three times for "opaque" and four to go back to "easy"). Figure 2 shows an example of what the annotation process looked like.
The scale aimed to capture increasing levels of difficulty, from familiar to entirely opaque. All words of the text could be annotated, regardless of their part of speech. As a result, it was expected that most words would receive a score of 0. By contrast with the scales mentioned above, ours only used one level for easy words. This was to avoid asking participants to annotate too many words, as including two different levels for familiar words would have required annotators to consider every single word in a text.

4.1. Overview of the Results

Initially, the number of annotators per text was as follows: 13 for text B1_A, 5 for B2_A and 10 for B2_B (a few participants only annotated one text instead of two). However, we decided to discard any participation for which the total time spent on annotating a text and answering the questions was less than 60 seconds. As texts were between 432 and 564 words long and the average reading speed is about 250 words per minute, this seemed a more than reasonable threshold to enforce. Two annotations were thus discarded, from participants who spent 9.5 and 20.5 seconds on texts B1_A and B2_B respectively.

Table 1 provides some descriptive information about each text. On average, participants spent between 8 and 9 minutes on a task (annotation + questions), with a rather high level of variability between annotators. Every participant whose contribution was kept spent at least 2 minutes on a single task.

Texts	B1_A	B2_A	B2_B
Annotators	12	5	9
Number of words	432	564	448
% Easy	97.22	98.23	97.77
% Transparent	1.85	1.06	1.34
% Vague	0.93	0.35	0.22
% Opaque	0	0.35	0.67
Average task time (s)	521.9	557.4	508
Standard deviation (s)	180	156	234

Table 1: Descriptive statistics for annotated texts.

The percentages provided for each level of difficulty were calculated based on the mean score attributed to each word. As possible values ranged from 0 (no annotation) to 3 (opaque word), we chose the following thresholds for each level: 0-0.74 (easy), 0.75-1.49 (transparent), 1.5-2.24 (vague) and 2.25-3 (opaque). Those ranges were selected to separate the space into four equal parts, and were only used to provide an idea of the distribution of difficult words. There does not seem to be any noticeable difference between the three texts, although one could have expected the two B2 texts to have a lower proportion of easy words. However, the average difficulty value of words that received a label other than 0 from at least one participant is slightly higher in the more advanced texts: 0.59 (*sd*: 0.56) for B1_A, 0.76 (*sd*: 0.71) for B2_A, and 0.84 (*sd*: 0.76) for B2_B.

4.2. Inter-Rater Agreement

For each text, an inter-rater agreement analysis was carried out using Krippendorff's α for ordinal values (Krippendorff, 2011). The results are presented in table 2.

The values obtained in this study are significantly higher than the one reported for the 2016 edition of the CWI task (0.244, (Paetzold and Specia, 2016)), which could be due to the fact that the group of annotators was more homogeneous. However, major differences between the two experiments make comparison somewhat tricky. For one, the datasets used in both studies differ considerably in size: over 230,000 words were annotated by 400 participants in the 2016 task (Paetzold and Specia, 2016), for about 1,500 words and 16 annotators in the present pilot study. Although Krippendorff's α for ordinal data is less sensitive to the number of coders than other inter-rater agreement metrics (Antoine et al., 2014), such a difference in size cannot be overlooked. Moreover, the 2016 CWI dataset only included content words and was annotated in a binary manner, while this study made all words annotable and used a 4-point complexity scale.

Texts	B1_A	B2_A	B2_B
Raters	12	5	9
Krippendorff's α	0.45	0.50	0.57
Binary α	0.45	0.50	0.57

Table 2: Inter-rater agreement per text; comparatively high values show the benefits of taking demographic data into account.

By contrast, the study carried out by Tack (2021) is much more similar to this one and should therefore allow comparisons to be made: inter-rater agreement scores were computed for groups of 8 to 17 participants, and all words of the texts could be annotated. As mentioned in section 2, a similar score to the one reported by Paetzold and Specia (2016) was achieved by the group of 9 participants with diverse L1 backgrounds, while agreement rates ranging from 0.36 to 0.51 were obtained for the four groups made up of more homogeneous profiles. The agreement rates computed for the present pilot study confirm the finding that annotators with a similar profile produce congruent difficulty judgements. Converting the difficulty levels to binary labels (any value higher than 0 is set to 1) in our data to more closely match the settings of Tack's study had almost no impact on the agreement scores, as shown in table 2. This can be explained by the fact that having fewer possible labels makes agreement by chance between annotators more likely, and goes to show that, as suggested by (Antoine et al., 2014), the weighted nature of Krippendorff's α makes it less sensitive to the number of coding categories than other metrics.

4.3. Link Between Proportion of Difficult Words and Global Text Comprehension

The question of whether there was a correlation between the annotation provided by a participant and their performance when answering comprehension questions was explored using Spearman's rank correlation coefficient. This non-parametric measure was used as the data did not follow a normal distribution. The results are presented in table 3.

Two variables were tested for correlation with the num-

Texts	B1_A	B2_A	B2_B
Difficult x Correct	0.69	-0.11	0.13
Time x Correct	-0.08	0.72	-0.16

Table 3: Spearman's correlation tests (ρ).

ber of questions answered correctly by a participant: the proportion of words annotated as difficult (score of 1, 2 or 3) and the time spent on the task. The hypotheses were that 1) annotators who had found more words difficult would have a harder time answering the comprehension questions and 2) participants who spent more time on the annotation task would answer more questions correctly. In other words, we expected to find a negative correlation between percentage of annotated words and number of correct answers, and a positive correlation between time spent and number of correct answers.

Most of the results were inconclusive, and did not seem to support our hypotheses. The seemingly high positive correlation between the amount of time spent doing the task and the number of correct answers for text B2_A was not statistically significant (p = 0.086), probably due to the annotator pool being too small. Interestingly, a significant positive correlation was found between the proportion of difficult words and the number of correct answers for text B1_A ($p < 0.01$ with a one-tailed test going against our initial hypothesis). The same trend was found when aggregating all data, with a smaller but still significant positive correlation between the two variables (Spearman's ρ: 0.35, $p = 0.042$). This perhaps surprising result could be due to the fact that participants who completed the task more rigorously found a higher number of words to annotate. Indeed, a Spearman test between the time spent annotating a text and the proportion of words annotated as difficult found a small positive correlation between the two - however, it was not significant (Spearman's ρ: 0.23, $p = 0.134$).

It is worth noting that none of the annotators found more than 5% of the words of each text difficult (max: 4.63%). This implies that all participants were over the vocabulary coverage threshold of 95% that Laufer and Ravenhorst-Kalovski (2010) argue is required in order to understand a text properly. It is therefore likely that the positive correlation only holds true past a certain threshold, and that the trend would have been reversed had some participants found a higher proportion of the words of a given text difficult.

5. Conclusion and Future Work

The results presented in section 4 only scratched the surface as regards the types of exploratory analyses which could be undertaken using the tool. Data collected with it could also be fed to a predictive model, as was done during the shared tasks mentioned in section 2. Researchers could then make use of the demographic information that they are encouraged to gather in order to produce personalised predictions of difficulty.

The design of the tool aimed to address the shortcomings of previous approaches, namely the use of binary annotation data, the focus almost solely on English, and the low inter-rater agreement due to great heterogeneity in the pool of annotators. PADDLe is currently being used to gather data for a master's dissertation, which should further demonstrate the value of the interface.

Bibliographical References

Antoine, J.-Y., Villaneau, J., and Lefeuvre, A. (2014). Weighted Krippendorff's alpha is a more reliable metrics for multi-coders ordinal annotations: experimental studies on emotion, opinion and coreference annotation. In *Proceedings of the 14th Conference of the European Chapter of the Association for Computational Linguistics*, pages 550–559, Gothenburg, Sweden, April. Association for Computational Linguistics.

Coady, J., (1996). *L2 vocabulary acquisition through extensive reading*, page 225–237. Cambridge Applied Linguistics. Cambridge University Press.

Gooding, S. and Kochmar, E. (2018). CAMB at CWI shared task 2018: Complex word identification with ensemble-based voting. In *Proceedings of the Thirteenth Workshop on Innovative Use of NLP for Building Educational Applications*, pages 184–194, New Orleans, Louisiana, June. Association for Computational Linguistics.

Huckin, T. and Coady, J. (1999). Incidental vocabulary acquisition in a second language: A review. *Studies in Second Language Acquisition*, 21:181 – 193.

Krippendorff, K. (2011). Computing krippendorff's alpha-reliability.

Laufer, B. and Ravenhorst-Kalovski, G. C. (2010). Lexical threshold revisited: Lexical text coverage, learners' vocabulary size and reading comprehension. *Reading in a Foreign Language*, 22:15–30.

Paetzold, G. and Specia, L. (2016). SemEval 2016 task 11: Complex word identification. In *Proceedings of the 10th International Workshop on Semantic Evaluation (SemEval-2016)*, pages 560–569, San Diego, California, June. Association for Computational Linguistics.

Shardlow, M., Evans, R., Paetzold, G. H., and Zampieri, M. (2021a). SemEval-2021 task 1: Lexical complexity prediction. In *Proceedings of the 15th International Workshop on Semantic Evaluation (SemEval-2021)*, pages 1–16, Online, August. Association for Computational Linguistics.

Shardlow, M., Evans, R., and Zampieri, M. (2021b). Predicting lexical complexity in english texts. *CoRR*.

Sugiyama, K. (2017). Analyse de la compétence lexicale dans la compréhension écrite des apprenants japonais en français. *Revue japonaise de didactique du français, numéro spécial : Actes du IVe Congrès régional de la Commission Asie-Pacifique*, page 502 (12p.).

Tack, A. (2021). *Mark My Words! On the Automated Prediction of Lexical Difficulty for Foreign Language Readers*. Ph.D. thesis.

Wesche, M. B. and Paribakht, T. S. (1996). Assessing second language vocabulary knowledge: Depth versus breadth. *Canadian Modern Language Review-Revue Canadienne Des Langues Vivantes*, 53:13–40.

Yimam, S. M., Štajner, S., Riedl, M., and Biemann, C. (2017). CWIG3G2 - complex word identification task across three text genres and two user groups. In *Proceedings of the Eighth International Joint Conference on Natural Language Processing (Volume 2: Short Papers)*, pages 401–407, Taipei, Taiwan, November. Asian Federation of Natural Language Processing.

Yimam, S. M., Biemann, C., Malmasi, S., Paetzold, G., Specia, L., Štajner, S., Tack, A., and Zampieri, M. (2018). A report on the complex word identification shared task 2018. In *Proceedings of the Thirteenth Workshop on Innovative Use of NLP for Building Educational Applications*, pages 66–78, New Orleans, Louisiana, June. Association for Computational Linguistics.

Proceedings of the 2nd READI Workshop @ LREC2022, pages 54–61
Marseille, 24 June 2022

Open corpora and toolkit for assessing text readability in French

Nicolas Hernandez, Nabil Oulbaz, Tristan Faine
LS2N, Nantes Université
France
nicolas.hernandez@ls2n.fr, {nabil.oulbaz,tristan.faine}@etu.univ-nantes.fr

Abstract

Measuring the linguistic complexity or assessing the readability of written productions has been the concern of several researchers in pedagogy and (foreign) language teaching for decades. The children's language development and the second language (L2) learning are in focus with tasks such as age or reader's level recommendation, or text simplification. Despite the interest for the topic, open datasets and toolkits for processing French are scarce. In this paper, we present: (1) three new open corpora for supporting research on readability assessment in French, (2) a dataset analysis with traditional formulas and an unsupervised measure, (3) a toolkit dedicated for French processing which includes the implementation of statistical formulas, a pseudo-perplexity measure, and state-of-the-art classifiers based on MLP, SVM, fastText and fine-tuned CamemBERT for predicting readability levels, and (4) an evaluation of the toolkit on the three data sets.

Keywords: open-source, free, corpus, toolkit, readability assessment, French

1. Introduction

Text readability refers to the difficulty in understanding a given text. The difficulty depends on the reader's language ability and knowledge background as well as the linguistic complexity of the written object. Measuring the linguistic complexity or assessing the readability of spoken or written productions has been the concern of several researchers in pedagogy and (foreign) language teaching for decades. Children's language development (Blandin et al., 2020) or second language (L2) learning (Yancey et al., 2021) are mainly in focus with tasks such as age or reader's level recommendation (Rahman et al., 2020; Pintard and François, 2020), or text simplification (Javourey-Drevet et al., 2022).

Works on readability assessment can be classified into three approaches: (1) the statistical formulas, (2) the language model (LM)-based measures, and (3) the supervised approaches. The latter can be categorised further into two types: (3a) the (linguistic) feature-based and (3b) the deep learning-based approaches.

The formulas (1) are often called traditional because they correspond to early works in the field (Gunning, 1971; Smith and Senter, 1967; Kincaid et al., 1975; Mc Laughlin, 1969). Despite the fact they do not capture all the linguistic complexity of the discourse, they have the advantage to be easily implementable. The LM-based approaches (2) benefit from being unsupervised. With the advent of deep learning in especially Natural Language Processing (NLP), the LMs switch from statistical to neural ones (Martinc et al., 2021). They can be considered as formulas' evolution. The feature-based approaches (3a) were the standard approaches before deep learning became the new reference of doing machine learning (Balakrishna, 2015; Wilkens et al., 2022; Crossley et al., 2022). In practice, they remain quite competitive for readability tasks with end-users because they offer explicability and concrete (linguistic) objects that humans can discuss and understand. Deep neural architectures have been proposed to support the prediction of readability classes (Azpiazu and Pera, 2019b; Deutsch et al., 2020; Rahman et al., 2020; Martinc et al., 2021; Yancey et al., 2021). Works at the edge attempt to combine the advantage of a feature-based approach with a deep learning one (Deutsch et al., 2020; Qiu et al., 2021).

Despite the interest for the field, resources for processing French are scarce, while open datasets and toolkits exist in other languages. Free implementations of the readability formulas exist for processing English[1]. Linguistic feature-based approaches are also available as open source libraries for computing readability metrics in English[2] (Balakrishna, 2015) and in Portuguese.[3] The implementation of (Martinc et al., 2021)'s neural approaches have been proposed for German readability assessment[4] while Deutsch et al. (2020) and Qiu et al. (2021) released their code with the paper respectively for processing English and Chinese. The study of English is also supported by the availability of several corpora (Vajjala and Meurers, 2012; Vajjala and Lučić, 2018). Recently Crossley et al. (2022) initiated the creation of an open corpus in English.

In terms of toolkit for processing French, the CENTAL Lab. offers AMesure,[5] an on-line demonstration application to analyse lexical, syntactic and textual difficulties of French administrative texts and rate the readability with a scale from 1 to 5 (François et al., 2018). Recently, the CENTAL has deployed another

[1]`https://github.com/cdimascio/py-readability-metrics`
[2]`https://bitbucket.org/nishkalavallabhi/complexity-features`
[3]`https://github.com/vwoloszyn/pylinguistics`
[4]`https://github.com/kinimod23/GRANT`
[5]`https://cental.uclouvain.be/amesure`

web service called FABRA[6] to assess reading difficulty in French. The toolkit is based on the aggregation of several linguistic features (Wilkens et al., 2022). Based on fine-tuning BERT on texts from French as a Foreign Language (FFL) course material following the Common European Framework of Reference for Languages (CEFR), (Yancey et al., 2021) will offer a web interface[7] for readability evaluation. Without discussing the performance of these deployed analysers, the quality of a toolkit as a service will depend on both the bandwidth availability and the power of the server. In addition, it will act as a blackbox and will not allow modification. Although there are nice projects funded by the National French Agency such as texttokids[8], there are little corpora freely available yet. We can mention the works of (Gala et al., 2020) and (Azpiazu and Pera, 2019a) who make available French corpora with aligned original and simplified texts. Our contributions are:

1. (1) three open corpora for supporting research on readability assessment in French,
2. (2) a dataset analysis with traditional formulas and an unsupervised measure,
3. (3) a toolkit dedicated for French processing which includes the implementation of statistical formulas, a pseudo-perplexity measure, and state-of-the-art classifiers based on multi-layer perceptron (MLP), Support Vector Machine (SVM), fastText and fine-tuned BERT for predicting readability levels,
4. and (4) an evaluation of the toolkit on the three data sets.

The library and corpora will be made available under open license in a repository later on.
The rest of the paper is structured as follows: Section 2 introduces the related work on readability measures and prediction techniques. We also say a few words on the grades system in France. Section 3 presents the corpora we collected for supporting readability studies and recommendation or prediction tasks. Section 4 presents a thorough analysis of our corpora as well as the report of the results of state-of-the art prediction systems.

2. Related Work

The readability assessment issue has been addressed by several researchers trying to find pertinent factors to take into account in order to automate this task. Martinc et al. (2021) offer a consolidated review of the major approaches.

[6]https://cental.uclouvain.be/fabra
[7]https://cental.uclouvain.be/amesure
[8]https://texttokids.irisa.fr/project

2.1. Traditional formulas

Readability measures mentioned in this section refer to methods based on mathematical functions linking text structural characteristics to a simple value of readability as perceived by humans. The structural characteristics are statistical measures on each text such as total words, total sentences, number of long words and number of syllables.

The Gunning fog index (GFI) formula (Gunning, 1971) takes into consideration the total number of words and sentences and the number of long words (long words are defined as words longer than 7 characters). GFI value and readability are negatively correlated meaning that a high GFI value indicates a higher readability measure. The Automated readability index (ARI) formula (Smith and Senter, 1967) corresponds to the number of study years needed to understand a text. It uses as features, similar to GFI, the total number of words and sentences in a text with the addition of the total number of characters. The Flesch reading ease (FRE) formula (Kincaid et al., 1975) brings an addition to the already mentioned formulas. It uses total number of syllables in a text to compute a score that increases with more readable documents. The Flesch-Kincaid grade level (FKGL) (Kincaid et al., 1975) is a similar formula to FRE, it corresponds to the number of years of education needed to understand a certain text. The Simple Measure of Gobbledygook (SMOG) formula (Mc Laughlin, 1969) similar to FKGL and ARI returns the number of years of education required to understand a text. It uses the number of polysyllables - the number of words containing three or more syllables in a text. Flesch's reading ease has been adapted to French language by (Kandel and Moles, 1958). They made changes to the coefficients of FRE to take into account the length difference between French and English Words. Their formula is named Reading Ease Level (REL).

2.2. Language model-based measures

Perplexity (ppl) is a common intrinsic metric for evaluating language models. It is defined as the exponential average negative log-likelihood of a sequence. For masked language models like BERT (Devlin et al., 2018), Salazar et al. (2020) proposed an adaptation called the pseudo-perplexity (pppl). The lower the score is the better the language model is able to "predict" a given text.
Martinc et al. (2021) also proposed a ranked sentence readability score (RSRS) which exploits language models to estimate a readability score for each word in a specific context.

2.3. Supervised approaches

Many traditional machine learning algorithms were experimented for the readability prediction task (Schwarm and Ostendorf, 2005; Vajjala and Meurers,

2012). These methods used various kind of features: traditional formulas scores, discourse cohesion measures, lexico-semantic features, syntactic and language model measures. The literature reveals that Support Vector Machine (SVM) classifier was giving the best results for (Martinc et al., 2021).
Feature-based approaches are language and genre-dependent. With the success encountered by Deep Learning methods for tackling numerous NLP tasks, end-to-end neural architectures were also proposed for difficulty estimation or readability classification.
Filighera et al. (2019) designed architectures comprising three global layers: an input layer made of contextual and non-contextual word embeddings (word2vec (Mikolov et al., 2013), BERT (Devlin et al., 2018), ...), an intermediate layer dedicated to the building of a text representation (thanks to Bi-LSTM or CNN layers), than a final dense layer to perform the prediction. Martinc et al. (2021) proposed a classifier by fine-tuning a pre-trained BERT model on a specific readability corpus. This latter approach correspond to the state-of-the-art performances. This approach gave the best results in Yancey et al. (2021) in a CEFR classification task of French as a foreign language.

2.4. Ages, grades, readability levels...

Age	Cat.	LC	FR grade	CEFR	US grade
<6	Pre.	lc1	PS, MS, GS		Kinder.
6-9	Prim.	lc2	CP, CE1, CE2	A1	1-3
9-12	Prim., Sec.	lc3	CM1, CM2, 6e	A1-A2	4-6
12-15	Sec.	lc4	5e, 4e, 3e	A2-B1	7-9
15-18	High		2nd, 1st, terminal	B1-B2	9-12

Table 1: Alignment of age, grades in French (FR) and in US, French learning cycle (LC), category (Cat.) such as Preschool (Pre.), Primary (Prim.), Secondary (Sec.) and High School, Kindergarten, and the Common European Framework of Reference for Languages (CEFR).

Since 2014, the French primary school (*primaire*) has been split into four learning cycles[9]. To erase any maturity differences, the learner has 3 years to acquire the required skills before the next stage: cycle 1 "first learning" (under 6, PS-GS), cycle 2 "fundamental learning" (6-8, CP-CE2), cycle 3 "consolidation" (9-11, CM1-6e) and cycle 4 "enhancement" (12-14, 5e-3e). At the primary school, the reading levels follows this development.
In order to provide a basis for recognising language qualifications, the Council of Europe proposed to "organise language proficiency in six levels, which can be regrouped into three broad levels: Basic User (beginner A1, intermediate A2), Independent User (B1, B2) and Proficient User (C1, C2)" called the The Common European Framework of Reference for Languages (CEFR).[10]A1 corresponds to beginner at primary school, A2 to intermediate at secondary school, B1 to newly independent at the end of the compulsory education (*collège*), B2 to advanced at high school (*baccalauréat*), C1 to autonomous learner, C2 to master.
Table 1 attempts to provide an overview of the alignment between the ages, grades and the education syllabus.

3. Datasets

Our datasets result from the compilation of various sources releasing children's and young adult's books under open licences (mainly in CC BY). These include the following projects: *littérature de jeunesse libre*, *StoryWeaver*, *Bibebook*, *Je Lis Libre*, WikiSource and Gutenberg. Some of these sources are collecting and packaging books coming from other sources. For more convenience, we will refer here to three distinct packages: *littérature de jeunesse libre (ljl)*, *Bibebook (bb)* and *Je Lis Libre (jll)*. Books belong to the literary genre (children story, adventure novel, poetry, theatre play...). The *littérature de jeunesse libre (ljl)*[11] corpus compiles children's books acquired from the StoryWeaver platform which defines four reading levels:[12] (lv1) beginning to read (easy words with repetition, short sentences, up to 250 words), (lv2) learning to read (simple concepts, from 250 to 600 words), (lv3) reading independently (popular topics with well sketched-out characters, 600 to 1500), (lv4) reading proficiently (rich vocabulary, word play, more than 1500 words). In our interpretation, we consider lv1 and lv2 covering the second learning cycle (lc2), and lv3 and lv4 covering the third one (lc3). Books are mainly children stories translated from Hindi or African literature. The 746 books were written by 460 distinct authors.
With the *bibebook (bb)* project, the Association de Promotion de l'Ecriture et de la Lecture (APEL) aims at promoting writing and reading activities for young adults. The corpus references books[13] that are in the public domain (i.e. with authors who died more than 70 years ago), and which are known as classic masterpieces that young adults read in French secondary

[9]Loi d'orientation sur l'éducation de 1989, modifiée en 2014 par un décret de 2013 `https://www.education.gouv.fr/bo/13/Hebdo32/MENE1318869D.htm?cid_bo=73449`

[10]`https://www.coe.int/en/web/common-european-framework-reference-languages`

[11]`litterature-jeunesse-libre.fr/bbs/`

[12]`storyweaver.org.in/reading_levels`

[13]`www.bibebook.com/visual-search?f%5B0%5D=field_genre%3A1267`

school (such as La Fontaine's tales, Molière's plays, Vernes's adventure novels, Zola's novels, Racine's plays). Books are organised in three levels of difficulty: easy reading (age 10-12), intermediate reading (12-15), and advanced reading (15-18). The 208 books are written by 72 distinct authors.
The *je lis libre*[14] project is a small database which refers to a subset of books present in *bibebook* database. The organisation is different and follows the reading recommendation from the Ministry of Education for a given secondary school grade: grades from 6 to 3 (3 being higher than 6 in the French education system).
To collect the books, we scrapped each website (while respecting the `robots.txt` restrictions) to get the pdf or epub files of each document, and used common tools, such as the pdftotext python library [15] to convert them into text format. Thanks to adhoc filters or manual operations, we were able to clean them as much as possible by removing meta-data descriptions (header and footer).
Dataset statistics are presented in Table 2. Sentence splitting and word tokenization were performed thanks to the NLP `spaCy` library and its `fr_core_news_sm`[16] model.
When looking at the number of tokens or the number of documents for each readability class, we clearly see that the corpora are unbalanced. We can also note that the corpora are small in terms of number of documents while being big in terms of number of sentences and tokens. We do not report here the average number of tokens per document but we can easily infer from the Table that the document size in the *ljl* corpus goes from 150 to 1,500 words approximately, and to tens of thousands of words in the *bb* and *jll* corpora.
The vocabulary size for *ljl* corpus is 23,123 words, 36,011 for *jll* and 38,503 for *bb*. The latter two are somewhat comparable, however the *ljl* corpus is lacking diversity in its words.

4. Datasets analysis and class prediction

In this section, we report:

- First the readability analysis of our corpora thanks to the traditional formulas and the pseudo-perplexity measure (cf. Section 4.1) ;
- Then we evaluate baseline approaches over the corpora and provide preliminary results for the class prediction task (cf. Section 4.2).

In both studies, we did not use the raw versions of the corpora. For each corpus, due to the imbalance between the classes, the size of the documents and the small number of documents we have at our disposal for each class, we decided to artificially generate new documents (d') from the big ones. New documents were generated to be between 140 and 200 words, with all beginning and ending not starting or ending in the middle of sentences. In (Crossley et al., 2022), the authors did the same to build up their corpus. The distinction is that our generation is automatic and consequently our generated documents may not correspond to an idea unit. For the *ljl* corpus, the strategy was to split the big documents into smaller pieces while for *bb* and *jll*, which comes with much larger documents, the strategy was to select text excerpts. We could not get smaller pieces with the *ljl* corpus. For the *bb* and *jll* corpora, we generated documents to obtain about 1k of documents per class. The number of generated documents remains proportional to the number of actual documents.
Last column of Table 2 indicates the number of generated documents.

R_{class}	$\#d$	$\#s$	$\#t$	$\#d'$
littérature de jeunesse libre (ljl)				
lv1	240	4,880	38,976	240
lv2	314	13,049	128,019	628
lv3	134	10,354	124,901	670
lv4	58	7,743	101,165	522
Bibebook (bb)				
easy	52	285,339	4,391,733	988
interm.	91	54,465	857,645	1,729
advan.	65	507,049	8,099,112	1,253
Je Lis Libre (jll)				
6e	13	57,399	1,349,523	1,285
5e	12	50,664	960,218	1,187
4e	10	87,234	1,616,076	989
3e	9	33,414	475,616	890

Table 2: Dataset statistics with readability class (R_{class}), number of documents (#d), of sentences (#s), of tokens (#t), and the number of artificial documents (#d'). The readability classes follow an increasing order: $lv1 < lv2 < lv3 < lv4$, $easy < interm. < advan$ and $6e < 5e < 4e < 3e$.

4.1. Dataset analysis

Table 3 reports the scores given by the traditional formulas and the pseudo-perplexity measure presented respectively in Section 2.1 and 2.2. The scores were averaged over all the documents of a given class. The *pppl* measure was computed by using the generative GPT model `gpt-fr-cased-small`.[17] For each measure, we calculated the Pearson coefficient ($p - score$) in order to estimate the linear correlation between these values and the levels labeled in each corpus.
Regarding the *ljl* corpus, the computed scores of each measure match the classes: The higher a readability class is, the higher the scores are. This is translated into a positive Pearson correlation score except for the

[14] `www.crdp-strasbourg.fr/je_lis_libre`
[15] `https://github.com/jalan/pdftotext`
[16] `https://spacy.io/models/fr`

[17] Sourced by `https://huggingface.co/asi`

R_{class}	GFI	ARI	FRE	FKGL	SMOG	REL	PPPL
littérature de jeunesse libre (ljl)							
lv1	44.61	14.12	78.6	4.28	15.97	94.38	54.59
lv2	66.88	19.8	67.61	6.32	18.65	84.55	57.79
lv3	91.21	25.66	59.04	8.06	21.11	76.81	63.80
lv4	105.52	27.87	54.92	8.81	22.15	73.81	62.87
p-score	0.48	0.49	-0.40	0.45	0.49	-0.40	0.04
Bibebook (bb)							
easy	122.6	35.56	57.04	9.42	23.85	74.49	152.33
interm.	128.93	36.71	56.04	9.67	24.06	73.56	414.00
advan.	122.6	36.26	58.03	9.38	23.95	75.30	161.62
p-score	-0.003	0.012	0.021	-0.006	0.005	0.019	-0.007
Je Lis Libre (jll)							
6e	119.82	46.38	77.38	7.96	23.74	91.45	177.68
5e	132.39	40.75	60.49	9.53	24.38	77.17	114.06
4e	102.42	36.12	81.63	6.27	21.69	95.73	172.71
3e	104.06	34.36	79.84	6.24	21.12	94.32	169.45
p-score	-0.11	-0.19	0.12	-0.17	-0.19	0.13	0.02

Table 3: Traditional formulas and pseudo-perplexity scores for all the readability class (R_{class}) of each corpus. The Pearson coefficient shows the correlation between the scores and the classes.

FRE measure since lower scores indicate that a text is less readable (negative $p-score$). We observe also that despite a positive increment, the lv3 and lv4 classes are closer than each of the other class pairs. This can indicate some difficulties to differentiate between them.

Looking at the *bb* and *jll* corpora, there is no significant correlation between the scores and their respective classes. We note, however, that for both corpora, the measures depict a peak in difficulty for the intermediate classes (namely the "intermediate" class in *bb* and the "5e" class in *jll*. In addition, the small deviation between the scores of the "4e" and the "3e" classes in the *jll* corpus seems to indicate there is no clear difference between the classes.

Concerning the pseudo-perplexity scores, the Pearson coefficient does not detect any correlation with the readability classes. But the *pppl* seems to confirm the closeness in the language of the lv3 and lv4 classes of the *ljl* corpus. It also confirms that the intermediate classes of the *bb* and *jll* corpora seem to follow an unexpected behaviour.

While in primary school the guideline is to pursue the children's development and to increase iteratively the linguistic complexity of the text, it seems that the reading recommendations in secondary school does not follow the same objective. Indeed the pedagogical choices are often to follow an historical progression, from old written texts to more contemporary ones.

Further observations of the corpus are necessary to clarify these numbers.

4.2. Readability class prediction

The current section reports the results obtained with four baselines over the three corpora for a class prediction task. The baselines differ from the text representation and the learning and classification algorithm. Two baselines are feature-based approaches and rely directly on words. One is based on non-contextual subword embeddings; it is fastText (Joulin et al., 2016). And the last one is based on contextual embeddings; it is BERT (Devlin et al., 2018).

4.2.1. Classifiers

In practice, thanks to the `scikit-learn`[18] library, we experimented several traditional machine learning algorithms (SVM, Random Forest, Logistic regression, multinomial Naive Bayes and multi-layer perceptron (MLP)) with normalised (or not) bag-of-words and TF-IDF text representations. We report only the very best of these approaches, namely the SVM and the MLP classifiers with a TF-IDF representation without any text normalisation.

FastText is a word embedding method that is an extension of the word2vec model (Mikolov et al., 2013). Instead of learning vectors for words directly, fastText represents each word as sub-word character n-grams. This offers more robustness to deal with previously unseen words. A document vector is obtained by averaging the subword embeddings. For the classification task, a multinomial logistic regression is used, where the document vector corresponds to the features.

Unlike word2vec-like models, BERT provides contextual embeddings to represent the meaning of words in context. BERT benefits from a bidirectional architecture based on Transformers and their attention mechanism. BERT can easily be used for classification task by adding a supplement dense layer. Training BERT for a classification task results in fine-tuning a pretrained BERT model with an additional layer for the

[18] `https://scikit-learn.org`

(ljl)	lv1			lv2			lv3			lv4				
	P	R	F1	P	R	F1	P	R	F1	P	R	F1	Acc.	Macro F1
MLP	0.42	0.46	0.44	0.47	0.62	0.53	0.47	0.47	0.47	0.55	0.31	0.40	0.48	0.47
SVM	0.41	0.52	0.46	0.47	0.55	0.51	0.48	0.48	0.48	0.52	0.36	0.42	0.47	0.47
fastText	0.49	0.46	0.47	0.59	0.7	0.64	0.71	0.79	**0.75**	0.94	0.62	0.75	0.68	0.65
CamemBERT	0.77	0.46	**0.57**	0.69	0.72	**0.71**	0.7	0.75	0.72	0.74	0.78	**0.76**	**0.71**	**0.69**

(bb)	easy			intermediate			advanced				
	P	R	F1	P	R	F1	P	R	F1	Acc.	Macro F1
MLP	0.44	0.33	0.37	0.52	0.61	0.56	0.51	0.48	0.50	0.50	0.48
SVM	0.44	0.38	0.40	0.53	0.62	0.57	0.54	0.47	0.51	0.51	0.49
fastText	0.75	0.73	**0.74**	0.77	0.78	0.78	0.78	0.78	0.78	0.77	0.76
CamemBERT	0.71	0.71	0.71	0.83	0.8	**0.81**	0.8	0.84	**0.82**	**0.79**	**0.78**

(jll)	6e			5e			4e			3e				
	P	R	F1	P	R	F1	P	R	F1	P	R	F1	Acc.	Macro F1
MLP	0.63	0.79	0.70	0.80	0.63	0.70	0.42	0.37	0.39	0.55	0.57	0.56	0.50	0.59
SVM	0.58	0.80	0.67	0.76	0.61	0.68	0.41	0.32	0.36	0.51	0.48	0.50	0.57	0.55
fastText	0.93	0.89	0.88	0.96	0.9	**0.96**	0.81	0.82	0.8	0.97	0.95	0.81	0.84	0.77
CamemBERT	0.96	0.95	**0.96**	0.92	0.93	0.93	0.87	0.88	**0.87**	0.92	0.91	**0.92**	**0.92**	**0.92**

Table 4: Results on 'littérature de jeunesse libre' (ljl), 'Bibebook' (bb) and 'Je Lis Libre' (jll) corpora for the class prediction task. Best Accuracy, F1-score and Macro average F1-score values are in bold.

task. For our experiments, we used CamemBERT, a state-of-the-art language model for French (Martin et al., 2020). The implementations of the fastText and BERT classifiers were supported by the *ktrain* library (Maiya, 2020).

The evaluation of the algorithms is based on the precision, recall, F1-score, accuracy, macro average F1-score metrics. The reported results for MLP and SVM were obtained by cross validation by splitting each dataset into five folds. For fastText and CamemBERT, the scores were obtained by averaging the scores over five runs, eachone with a randomly selected dataset with 90% for training and 10% for validating. Optimal learning rate (lr) and number of epochs hyperparameters were set up by utilizing the following learning rate schedules: the triangular policy (Smith, 2015), the 1cycle policy (Smith, 2018), and SGDR Warm Restart (Loshchilov and Hutter, 2016). We began training with a maximum value for lr. This was set to 0.0001 for fastText and $2e^{-5}$ for CamemBERT.

4.2.2. Results

Table 4 presents the results respectively for the corpora *ljl*, *bb* and *jll*. The best models are fastText and CamemBERT. Both are competing with each other over the three corpora but CamemBERT slightly outperforms fastText. FastText remains competitive probably by taking advantage of of a vocabulary made of subwords. MLP and SVM achieve similar performance; SVM being better on the *ljl* and *bb* corpora.

For all the models we note that results are higher in the *jll* corpus than in the *bb* corpus. This may come from the fact that the task may be harder for the *bb* corpus since there is a larger number of documents and fewer number of classes to differentiate the documents. The lowest performance scores were obtained for the *ljl* corpus, but this may due to the size of the corpus which remains relatively small.

The difference of performance between the classes of a same corpus seem to match the imbalance in number of instances between the classes. This suggests that future experiments should benefit from taking into consideration class weights. In general, the results are not bad but there is room for improvement in particular on the prediction task on a very small corpus (i.e. the *ljl* corpus).

Despite the fact that the corpus and the number of classes were different, the results are consistent with the results of Yancey et al. (2021) who observed that best results were obtained with a fine-tuned CamemBERT model.

5. Conclusion

Supporting primary and secondary education and developing effective learning environments are part of the Unesco's open science recommendations and its Sustainable Development Goal 4 (SDG4).[19] What is noticeable about the modern age is the efforts for researchers to enable other peers to access to the data and tools they develop (Crossley et al., 2022; Wilkens et al., 2022). With this paper, we aim at contributing to the efforts. Our material contributions are three corpora and a library for assessing readability in French available

[19] `https://unesdoc.unesco.org/ark:/48223/pf0000259784`

under open licences[20].

There are prospects for improving and extending the current work. One major direction will be to deepen the data analysis and the assessment of the data quality. Indeed, the low correlation coefficients question the quality of the *bb* and *jll* corpora. We plan to use the distribution of the current measures to filter out the outliers and observe whether the correlation scores improve. These measures attempt to capture the lexical complexity as well the syntax complexity (with the pppl). In order to verify the reliability of these measures to distinguish the different classes, we will compute correlations with additional lexical complexity measures (for instance by computing the distribution of the Dubois-Buyse school lexicon (Ters et al., 1977) over the classes of each corpus) as well as complementary measures designed for capturing the semantic complexity and the discourse cohesion of the texts. One appealing aspect with such linguistic features is that they can support the implementation of readability measures which allow to build self-explanable systems. Eventually we will also manually annotate a sample of the corpus to confirm there is no issues in the way the texts have been categorised. The study of the classification errors may also allow to understand how to improve our datasets. Since the process of building documents is partially artificial, it is important to ensure that classifiers actually learn to distinguish between readability levels and not from hidden variables (such as authors, topics...). Attention will be paid to other datasets configurations to verify the independence of the classifiers to the variables.

Last, we plan to extend the corpora. Since the data annotated by Crossley et al. (2022) is available in numerous languages, we can study the possibility of transferring to French their manual annotation. New genres such as encyclopaedic textbooks[21] will be considered, this could allow us to compare texts written by children and texts written by adults for children.

6. Acknowledgements

We are grateful to the the anonymous reviewers for their valuable comments which will help us to pursue this work in a more "high quality" direction. This work was partially supported by the French *Agence Nationale de la Recherche*, within its *Programme d'Investissements d'Avenir*, with grant ANR-16-IDEX-0007.

[20] `https://github.com/nicolashernandez/READI-LREC22`

[21] `https://fr.wikimini.org` (written by children) and `https://fr.vikidia.org`

7. Bibliographical References

Azpiazu, I. M. and Pera, M. S. (2019a). Is cross-lingual readability assessment possible? *In press*, 1(1):1–18.

Azpiazu, I. M. and Pera, M. S. (2019b). Multiattentive recurrent neural network architecture for multilingual readability assessment. *Transactions of the Association for Computational Linguistics*, 7:421–436.

Balakrishna, S. V. (2015). *Analyzing TextComplexity and Text Simplification: Connecting Linguistics, Processing and Educational Applications*. Ph.D. thesis, Universität Tübingen.

Blandin, A., Lecorvé, G., Battistelli, D., and Étienne, A. (2020). Recommandation d'âge pour des textes (age recommendation for texts). In *Actes de la 6e conférence conjointe Journées d'Études sur la Parole (JEP, 33e édition), Traitement Automatique des Langues Naturelles (TALN, 27e édition), Rencontre des Étudiants Chercheurs en Informatique pour le Traitement Automatique des Langues (RÉCITAL, 22e édition). Volume 2 : Traitement Automatique des Langues Naturelles*, pages 164–171, Nancy, France, 6. ATALA et AFCP.

Crossley, S., Heintz, A., Choi, J. S., Batchelor, J., Karimi, M., and Malatinszky, A. (2022). A large-scaled corpus for assessing text readability. *Behavior Research Methods*, 16 March.

Deutsch, T., Jasbi, M., and Shieber, S. (2020). Linguistic features for readability assessment. In *Proceedings of the Fifteenth Workshop on Innovative Use of NLP for Building Educational Applications*. Association for Computational Linguistics.

Devlin, J., Chang, M.-W., Lee, K., and Toutanova, K. (2018). Bert: Pre-training of deep bidirectional transformers for language understanding.

Filighera, A., Steuer, T., and Rensing, C. (2019). Automatic text difficulty estimation using embeddings and neural networks. In *European Conference on Technology Enhanced Learning (EC-TEL)*, pages 335–348, Delft, The Netherlands. Springer.

François, T., Müller, A., Degryse, B., and Fairon, C. (2018). Amesure : une plateforme web d'assistance à la rédaction simple de textes administratifs. *Repères DoRiF*, 16 – Littératie et intelligibilité : points de vue sur la communication efficace en contexte plurilingue, novembre.

Gala, N., Tack, A., Javourey-Drevet, L., François, T., and Ziegler, J. C. (2020). Alector: A parallel corpus of simplified french texts with alignments of misreadings by poor and dyslexic readers. In *Language Resources and Evaluation for Language Technologies (LREC)*, Marseille, France, May.

Gunning, R. (1971). *The Technique of Clear Writing*. McGraw-Hill.

Javourey-Drevet, L., Dufau, S., François, T., Gala, N., Ginestié, J., and Ziegler, J. C. (2022). Simplification of literary and scientific texts to improve reading fluency and comprehension in beginning readers of French. *Applied Psycholinguistics*, pages 1–28, January.

Joulin, A., Grave, E., Bojanowski, P., and Mikolov, T. (2016). Bag of tricks for efficient text classification.

Kandel, L. and Moles, A. (1958). Application de l'indice de flesch à la langue francaise. *Cahiers Etudes de Radio-Télévision*, pages 253–274.

Kincaid, J. P., Fishburne, R. P., Rogers, R. L., and Chissom, B. S. (1975). Derivation of new readability formulas (automated readability index, fog count and flesch reading ease formula) for navy enlisted personnel. *Institute for Simulation and Training*.

Loshchilov, I. and Hutter, F. (2016). Sgdr: Stochastic gradient descent with warm restarts.

Maiya, A. S. (2020). ktrain: A low-code library for augmented machine learning. *arXiv preprint arXiv:2004.10703*.

Martin, L., Muller, B., Suárez, P. J. O., Dupont, Y., Romary, L., Éric de la Clergerie, Seddah, D., and Sagot, B. (2020). Camembert: a tasty french language model. In *Proceedings of the 58th Annual Meeting of the Association for Computational Linguistics*, pages 7203–7219, Online, July. Association for Computational Linguistics.

Martinc, M., Pollak, S., and Robnik-Šikonja, M. (2021). Supervised and unsupervised neural approaches to text readability. *Computational Linguistics*, 47(1):141–179, Mar.

Mc Laughlin, G. H. (1969). Smog grading-a new readability formula. *Journal of Reading*, 12(8):639–646.

Mikolov, T., Chen, K., Corrado, G., and Dean, J. (2013). Efficient estimation of word representations in vector space.

Pintard, A. and François, T. (2020). Combining expert knowledge with frequency information to infer CEFR levels for words. In *Proceedings of the 1st Workshop on Tools and Resources to Empower People with REAding DIfficulties (READI)*, pages 85–92, Marseille, France, May. European Language Resources Association.

Qiu, X., Chen, Y., Chen, H., Nie, J.-Y., Shen, Y., and Lu, D. (2021). Learning syntactic dense embedding with correlation graph for automatic readability assessment. In *Proceedings of the 59th Annual Meeting of the Association for Computational Linguistics and the 11th International Joint Conference on Natural Language Processing (Volume 1: Long Papers)*, pages 3013–3025, Online, August. Association for Computational Linguistics.

Rahman, R., Lecorvé, G., Étienne, A., Battistelli, D., Béchet, N., and Chevelu, J. (2020). Mama/papa, is this text for me? In *Proceedings of the 28th International Conference on Computational Linguistics*, pages 6296–6301, Barcelona, Spain (Online), December. International Committee on Computational Linguistics.

Salazar, J., Liang, D., Nguyen, T. Q., and Kirchhoff, K. (2020). Masked language model scoring. In *Proceedings of the 58th Annual Meeting of the Association for Computational Linguistics*. Association for Computational Linguistics.

Schwarm, S. and Ostendorf, M. (2005). Reading level assessment using support vector machines and statistical language models. In *Proceedings of the 43rd Annual Meeting of the Association for Computational Linguistics (ACL'05)*, pages 523–530, Ann Arbor, Michigan, June. Association for Computational Linguistics.

Smith, E. A. and Senter, R. (1967). Automated readability index. *AMRL-TR. Aerospace Medical Research Laboratories*, pages 1–14.

Smith, L. N. (2015). Cyclical learning rates for training neural networks.

Smith, L. N. (2018). A disciplined approach to neural network hyper-parameters: Part 1 – learning rate, batch size, momentum, and weight decay.

Ters, F., Mayer, G., and Reichenbach, D. (1977). L'échelle dubois-buyse d'orthographe usuelle française. *OCDL. 5e édition revue et corrigée*, 1.

Vajjala, S. and Lučić, I. (2018). OneStopEnglish corpus: A new corpus for automatic readability assessment and text simplification. In *Proceedings of the Thirteenth Workshop on Innovative Use of NLP for Building Educational Applications*, pages 297–304, New Orleans, Louisiana, June. Association for Computational Linguistics.

Vajjala, S. and Meurers, D. (2012). On improving the accuracy of readability classification using insights from second language acquisition. In *Proceedings of the Seventh Workshop on Building Educational Applications Using NLP*, pages 163–173, Montréal, Canada, June. Association for Computational Linguistics.

Wilkens, R., Alfter, D., Wang, X., Pintard, A., Tack, A., Yancey, K., and François, T. (2022). Fabra: French aggregator-based readability assessment toolkit. In *In Proceedings of the thirteenth international conference on language resources and evaluation (LREC 2022), (submited)*.

Yancey, K., Pintard, A., and François, T. (2021). Investigating readability of french as a foreign language with deep learning and cognitive and pedagogical features. *Lingue e Linguaggio*, 2021(2):229–258.

Proceedings of the 2nd READI Workshop @ LREC2022, pages 62–69
Marseille, 24 June 2022

MWE for Essay Scoring English as a Foreign Language

Rodrigo Wilkens*, **Daiane Seibert**[†], **Xiaoou Wang***, **Thomas François***
*Cental, IL&C, UCLouvain, [†]KU Leuven,
rodrigo.wilkens@uclouvain.be, daiane.seibert@student.kuleuven.be,
{xiaoou.wang, thomas.francois}@uclouvain.be

Abstract

Mastering a foreign language like English can bring better opportunities. In this context, although multiword expressions (MWE) are associated with proficiency, they are usually neglected in the works of automatic scoring language learners. Therefore, we study MWE-based features (i.e., occurrence and concreteness) in this work, aiming at assessing their relevance for automated essay scoring. To achieve this goal, we also compare MWE features with other classic features, such as length-based, graded resource, orthographic neighbors, part-of-speech, morphology, dependency relations, verb tense, language development, and coherence. Although the results indicate that classic features are more significant than MWE for automatic scoring, we observed encouraging results when looking at the MWE concreteness through the levels.

Keywords: multiword expression (MWE), MWE feature analysis, MWE concreteness, automatic essay scoring

1. Introduction

Mastering a foreign language has become increasingly important in everyday life. English proficiency, for example, is correlated to higher salaries (e.g., Boyd and Cao (2009; Pendakur and Pendakur (2007; Adamchik et al. (2019)). The increase of foreign language learners also implies an increasing number of participants in the proficiency tests, such as TOEFL and IELTS, which may impact the test cost (e.g. including the need for training new evaluators). Automated scoring makes assessing language proficiency more viable for large-scale tests, which may be mandatory if one wants to study abroad (Weigle, 2013). In addition, the feedback provided by automated scoring based on linguistic features can also provide valuable insights to facilitate language learning (Srichanyachon, 2012).

For English, various tools have been used to support the development of research on foreign language writing development. Some examples are Coh-Metrix (Graesser et al., 2004), L2 Syntactic Complexity Analyzer (Lu, 2010), CTAP (Chen and Meurers, 2016) and TAASSC (Kyle, 2016). Although these tools provide a myriad of functional language descriptors, they are hardly extensible. Also, they are usually based on token units or n-grams as words to build features. However, multiwords expressions raise numerous challenges in natural language processing, descriptive linguistics and foreign language acquisition due to their formulaic structure (Wray, 1999; Wray, 2002), unit at some level of description (Calzolari et al., 2002), and interpretation crossing word boundaries (Sag et al., 2002). MWEs include several subcategories, such as verb-noun combinations (e.g. *rock the boat* and *see stars*), verb-particle constructions (e.g. *take off* and *clear up*), lexical bundles (e.g. *I don't know whether*) and compound nouns (e.g. *cheese knife* and *rocket science*). Targeting English as a foreign language, MWE's importance is undeniable when considering its ubiquity in the discourse produced by native speakers. Moreover, a learner may be considered handicapped in a language without knowledge about MWE (Muraki et al., 2022). Glucksberg (1989) estimated that English native speakers produce about four multiwords per minute and Jackendoff (1997) identified that they likely have the same order of magnitude as a single word in the mental lexicon of native speakers.

Given the prevalence of MWEs in native speakers' speech, we investigate their impact on learners' proficiency prediction. We compare MWE metrics with classic linguistic ones commonly used to identify learner proficiency to achieve this goal. In particular, we focus on MWEs and their concreteness (i.e., degree of concreteness/abstraction of an MWE). The main contributions of this paper are the following: (1) profile of MWE concreteness usage across the different levels of the Common European Framework of Reference for Languages (CEFR); (2) analysis of the capacity of MWE scores to individually identify the level; and (3) comparison of these scores with classic scores used to predict learners' level.

This work is organized as follows: first, we shortly review the literature concerning the essay scoring focusing on English and linguistic descriptors in Section 2. In Section 3, we present the linguistic descriptors and corpus used in this work. Next, in Section 4, we evaluate the impact of MWE descriptors on the prediction of learners' proficiency. Finally, we conclude by discussing the results in Section 5.

2. Related Work

Approaches for automatic prediction of language proficiency are mostly based on machine learning. These can be broadly divided into deep learning-based and feature-based, the latter being more interpretable. We thus focus on feature-based approaches for facilitating the comparison with the MWE descriptors.

The features have been drawn from explorations of linguistic patterns in corpora. For example, Lan et al. (2022) showed that there is an association between the use of noun phrases and whether the author is an L1 or L2 user of English. The first language plays a vital role in the developmental trajectories, characterizing behavior, as discussed by Chen et al. (2021), who observed different developmental trajectories in learners whose L1 has clause subordination structures distinct from English. They may overuse or underuse certain grammatical structures depending on their CEFR level (Zilio et al., 2018). Errors, such as punctuation, spelling and verb tense, are significant in predicting specific CEFR levels (Ballier et al., 2019). Jung et al. (2019) demonstrate relevance regarding the conceptual similarity between paragraphs when comparing with the lexical diversity, familiarity and abstractness of the word. Some works also combined properties such as part-of-speech and n-grams (Yannakoudakis et al., 2011), the edit distance between errors and their corresponding target hypothesis (Tono, 2013), and syntactic, lexical, discourse and error features (Vajjala, 2018).Jung et al. (2019) showed that length-based features, specifically the number of words, are stronger predictors than the cohesion and syntactic complexity. However, they also emphasize that text length alone cannot be considered a good predictor of writing quality.

Moreover, despite the variety of language-based features studied, only a few studies have tried to test multi-dimensional models with several features to investigate how they are comparable (e.g. (Tack et al., 2017)). Corpus specificities may also bias studies. In EFCAMDAT (Geertzen et al., 2013), the task (i.e., the prompt[1]) presented in the test might drive the learner to use different skills, as discussed by Alexopoulou et al. (2017) and by Michel et al. (2019), who identified task influence by exploring lexical and syntactic features.

Despite the amount of work on language assessment, there is still a comparability gap in the results. In this sense, Ballier et al. (2020) called for solutions for predicting CEFR levels for written productions using only the French part of the EFCAMDAT. Competitors used a variety of machine learning approaches with different processes including feature engineering, data representation and classification. The winner, Balikas (2018), used Gradient Boosted Trees and compared the use of language models, part-of-speech, bag-of-words (BoW) and Latent Dirichlet Allocation (LDA) as features. Interestingly, their results of both BoW and LDA models were close. Arnold et al. (2018) use a multi-dimensional feature representation of written essays exploring LSTM and dense layers achieving an accuracy of 70%. Using EFCAMDAT texts written by French and Spanish learners, Gaillat et al. (2021) achieved an accuracy of 82% when exploring microsystems, identifying lexical and syntactic features as the more significant.

[1]Prompts are the proposed topics for the writing.

Focusing on MWE, the literature has reported different effects depending on their type. Römer (2019) and Römer and Berger (2019) studied the verb-argument construction (VCP) repertoire of English learners, remarking an increase in vocabulary, productivity and complexity according to learners' level. Du et al. (2022) studied collocation usage by English learners, using a list of 2,501 *make/take+noun (the direct object).* They observed that proficient learners tend to use collocations containing more semantically complicated and abstract nouns. Garner (2016) examined the use of p-frames[2] by L1 German learners of English as a foreign language, observing that p-frames in texts from higher proficiency learners are more variable, less predictable, and more functionally complex. Arnon and Snider (2010) explored the perceived transparency affected by multiword phrases (MWP; the specific combinations of words that occur together more than would be predicted by chance). For that, they compared *verb+object* phrase[3] knowledge among intermediate and advanced L2 English learners in comparison to monolingual L1 speakers, observing that intermediate learners performed less accurately and advanced learners performed comparably with native English on transparent and semi-transparent items but were less accurate for non-transparent items. Moreover, both intermediate and advanced learners answered non-transparent items less accurately than transparent items. Exploring MWE validity, Dahlmann and Adolphs (2007) studied pauses in various instances of very frequent extracted MWE candidates (i.g. n-grams) from a learner corpus. Arnon and Snider (2010) studied the frequency of four-word phrases using the distributional information, identifying an association between frequency and the identification as a valid MWE. Based on n-grams statistics, Jung et al. (2019) identified a correlation between their frequency and essay score.

3. Methodology

Considering the goal of investigating the impact of MWE usage on the prediction of learners' proficiency, we annotated a corpus of essays written by English learners with features describing MWE occurrence and its concreteness. We also annotate the corpus with additional features aiming to assess the importance of MWE features. After we have the annotated corpus, we run the tests described in Section 4.

We used EFCAMDAT (Geertzen et al., 2013), created by the University of Cambridge and Education First (EF) to supply the lack of data for numerous speakers across the proficiency spectrum and the amounts of annotated data. In total, it consists of +1M of essays across the 6 CEFR levels written by learners of

[2]P-frames are a type of semi-fixed word sequence in which fixed words surround an open slot (Stubbs, 2007).

[3]For example, break a bone (Transparent); break the silence (Semi-transparent); break the ice (Non-transparent).

198 nationalities. Levels and nationalities are not balanced (e.g. 40% of all texts are from Brazilians, and 53.04% and 0.16% of the texts are at levels A1 and C2, respectively). Therefore, we selected only the 10 most common nationalities and joined levels C1 and C2 due to their low representation in the corpus. We also truncated the number of essays using the level with the least essays by nationality. Table 3 presents the corpus size employed in this work, identifying the number of essays considered in each level for each nationality.

Nationality	Usage per level	Corpora (%)
Brazil	2469	22.99
Germany	2469	22.99
Italy	1238	11.53
Russia	1195	11.13
France	818	7.62
Mexico	762	7.09
China	555	5.17
Saudi Arabia	468	4.36
Japan	420	3.91
Taiwan	347	3.23

Table 1: Number of used texts for each nationality and its percentage in corpus used in this study.

For studying the impact of MWE on text produced by English learners, we explored 2 features:

1. MWE usage ($\mathbf{MWE_{cnt}}$) a list-based (Muraki et al., 2022) feature that consists of 62 thousand expressions from recommended expressions for learners, stimuli expressions used in language studies, dictionaries and n-grams frequency lists.

2. Concreteness of MWE (Muraki et al., 2022) $\mathbf{MWE_{conc}}$. In other words, how the 62 thousand MWE are perceived as concrete/abstract according to 2,825 participants (all English native speakers). [4] The provided annotation was cleaned by removing participants with less than 33% of the ratings and with low correlation with others. On average, each MWE received 10.4 valid scores (minimum of 10).

Aiming to compare these 2 features with others reported in the literature, we also employed 337 features. As some of them are close in terms of definition and represented phenomenon, we grouped them into 14 families of features.

Length-based features (**LEN**) count the word length (i.e., number of letters in a token and its stem, and the number of syllables) and the number of words per sentence. In total, 4 length-based features.

Graded resource features (**GRD**) contain normalized frequencies of word lemmas divided by level from EFLLex (Dürlich and François, 2018). We use a total of 6 features based on graded resources.

[4]Unfamiliar MWE were not annotated.

Frequency features (**FRQ**) consider the frequency of words in a reference corpus. In this work, we consider the frequency of all words in a text, only content words (i.e., nouns, proper nouns, verbs, adjectives and adverbs in the text), only functional words, only common nouns, only verbs and only adjective. As the reference corpus, we explored the total normalized frequency (ignoring levels) in EFLLex (Dürlich and François, 2018) and contextual diversity on SUBTLEX (Brysbaert and New, 2009). In sum, 18 frequency-based features.

Features based on orthographic neighbor (**NGH**) measure orthographic or phonetic similarity between words. In this work, we use the mean orthographic and phonologic Levenstein distances (Bartlett et al., 2009) and the absolute and average number of neighbors and their frequency (Brysbaert and New, 2009). Also, the occurrence and cumulative frequency of neighbors with higher frequency than the words in the text are used. In total, 8 features.

Lexical norms (**NRM**) features resort to the MRC database (Coltheart, 1981) to annotate age of acquisition, concreteness, familiarity and imageability of each word. In addition, we also identify the percentage of out-of-vocabulary in each of the four features.

Lexical sophistication (**SOP**) features identify the number of sophisticated tokens and types considering all words, content words, and verbs considering the surface form in Dale and Chall (1948). In sum, 6 features.

Moreover, we use syntactic annotation automatically extracted from the Stanza parser (Qi et al., 2020).[5] Part-of-speech tags (**POS**) are counted using. 17 tags described in the Universal POS tags are considered. Morphology features (**MOR**) target the morphological components of the words. As they operate in a lower level of the POS, we also use the Stanza parser for annotating the 56 features. Dependency relations (**DEP**) employ the 37 functions proposed by Universal Dependencies[6]. In addition, verb tense (**TNS**) features put together POS and morphology relations to identify the verb tenses as they are commonly taught. We use 19 verb tenses: simple tenses, perfect, continuous, emphatic and conditional tenses, and also the imperative, the tenses. All based on Stanza parser and identified through handcrafted rules. We also explore constituency parser (Kitaev et al., 2019) for extracting phrase (**PRH**) usage, differentiating 25 phrase types. In addition, we also count the number of phrases.

Language development (**DEV**) features include the Yngve index constituency parser (Yngve, 1960), number of words before and after the main verb, and the average phrase and sentence depth in the text. In total, 5 features related to language development.

Lexical diversity features (**DVR**) explore variations of type-token-ratio (TTR) that have been widely used for measuring language proficiency. In this

[5]We do not assess parser instabilities stability caused by learner errors, but Berzak et al. (2016) addressed the subject.

[6]https://universaldependencies.org/

work explored the Moving Average TTR (MATTR; (Covington and McFall, 2010)) with a window size of 100 words; Corrected TTR (CTTR; (Carroll, 1964)); Root TTR (RTTR; (Guiraud, 1959)); Bilogarithmic TTR (LogTTR; (Herdan, 1960; Herdan, 1966)); SquaredTTR (Chaudron and Parker, 1990); and UberIndex (Arnaud and Béjoint, 1992). For those, we distinguish between the ratios of lemmas and surface forms as well as all words, content words (i.e. nouns, proper nouns, verbs, adjectives, and adverbs in the text), adjective, adverb, adjective and adverb, nouns and pronouns, and verb. In addition, we specialized the verb features normalizing by the content words and verbs. In sum, we use 112 DVR features.

Coherence features (**COH**) use language models to compare the input text with the language's reference usage. We used ukWaC (Baroni et al., 2009), a 2 billion word corpus that covers a great range of themes, to train our models. Our first model, LSA, has 250 dimensions with stopwords and punctuations being removed and the 100,000 most frequent tokens/lemmas were kept. For the second model, PPMI, the dimension and window size were set to 500 and 2 without removing stopwords (Bullinaria and Levy, 2007). For these models, we calculate the cosine similarity of all pairs of adjacent sentences and the cosine similarity of each sentence with all the other sentences are computed (for the PPMI case, all the word vectors of a sentence are averaged). In total that makes 8 features. We also estimate the probability and perplexity of each sentence by training two 4-gram models on ukWaC (uncased tokens and lemmas) in the third model. This was created using KenLM (Heafield et al., 2013), a language modeling toolkit based on modified Kneser-Ney smoothing (Kneser and Ney, 1995). The n-gram model added 4 features. Finally, the fourth model, 3 features, is a simple n-gram frequency varying n between 2 and 4 on uncased and lemmatized ukWaC using SRILM (Stolcke, 2002), a language modeling toolkit.

4. Results

Following our goal, we analyze the MWE usage on the annotated corpus. We start by describing the MWE usage and concreteness in the corpus. This analysis allowed to draw a general profile of MWE in learners' essays (Section 4.1). Then, we focus on the applicability of MWE features for automatic essay scoring by investigating their correlation with the CEFR level (Section 4.2) and their applicability as features for a machine learning model (Section 4.3). We also compared the proposed features with the classic ones in the last two studies to evaluate their capacity to discriminate the levels.

4.1. Profiling MWE usage

The analysis of MWE usage by learners showed that 5.78% of the essays do not contain MWEs. In A1, A2 and B1 levels, there is an increase in the MWE usage, but they are similarly used at B2 and C.

The use of MWEs along the levels and the 128 prompts were also analysed. Prompts are specific per level, varying between 23 and 31 prompts. Only in the higher levels there are few occurrences of the same prompt shared in different levels (3% of the prompts). The quantity of essays is not the same for each prompt. A normalization considering the average of the prompts that had fewer documents was made to get a reliable result. Considering 2 standard deviations to the prompt to be an outlier, we observe two outlier prompts at A1, none at A2, one at B1 and B2, and three at C. For all levels, it corresponds to less than 10%.

The MWE' concreteness have a correlation of -0.11 with their usage per level. We observe that beginners are more familiar with more concrete MWEs and get used to more abstracted expressions as they go through the levels (concreteness average scores for A1-C are 3.1603, 3.0151, 2.7119, 2.5263 and 2.6087, respectively). Moreover, C level contains MWE present in the list but without annotated scores. It suggests that these MWEs are truly specific and indicative of a learner's high proficiency.

The skewness and kurtosis of the concreteness were also analysed per level (kurtosis is summarized in Figure 1). The concreteness distribution for A1 is flattened. As the level increases, the distribution approaches a normal distribution. The skewness, on the other hand, has low values for A1 and they increase across the levels, going from 0.0514 (A1) until 0.3966 (C)[7]. This suggests that the data has a positive deviation as the level increase, it means that the weight happens in the direction of the low scores of concreteness.

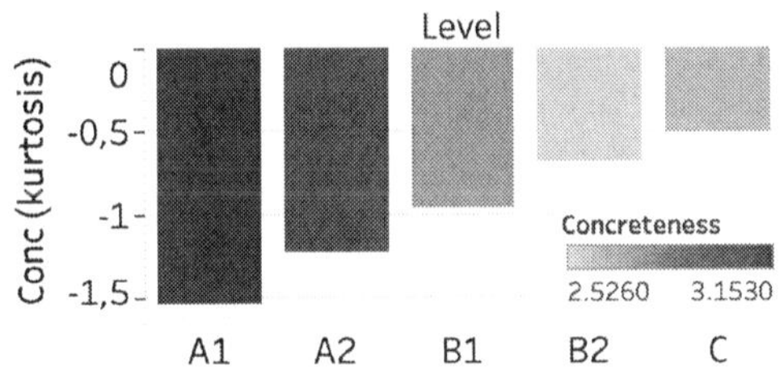

Figure 1: Concreteness kurtosis per level

4.2. Correlation

To study the relationship between the MWE and CEFR levels, we compared the Spearman correlation between MWE features and the level as well as all features described in Section 3. Those are summarized in Table 3 which shows the score most correlated with the level for each family of features presenting their rank and correlation considering the entire corpus and distinguishing by nationality. The table also shows the average rank and correlation of the features by family,

[7] A2 = 0.1572, B1 = 0.2607, B2 = 0.3519

considering the entire corpus, and by nationality; all correlations with p-value<0.05.

The top 40 features are predominantly related to lexical diversity. This result goes in the same direction as Jung et al. (2019). We also observed that the top 6 features have different ranks when nationality is considered. However, they are always in the top 6. Moreover, the top 1-3 are based on ratios considering all tokens, while and the top 4-6 are based on ratios of content words only. We also observed a band of features that alternate values between the top 7 and 16. Contrary to the pattern observed in the top 16 features, the features between 17 and 25 have almost constant rank across the nationalities. Below rank 25, we observed a considerable fluctuation in rank. This fluctuation can be seen in the standard deviation of the rank columns in Table 3.

We also analyzed the relation between the feature with the highest correlation and the average correlation for each family. As shown in Table 3, a higher correlated feature does not indicate that most of the features in their family are also highly correlated. For example, the SquaredTTR based on all tokens presented a correlation of 0.81 with the CEFR level, but in average the DVR features presented 0.42 as correlation. This indicates that only a few features are broadly meaningful for level identification. However, it does not mean that the other features may be ignored.

Targeting on MWE, their average concreteness is more correlated with the level than their usage (0.36 v. 0.21). In other words, the use of less concrete MWE is a better indication of a CEFR level than a higher number of MWE, although both features showed weak relationships with the level. Furthermore, we explored 18 statistics descriptors[8] to better describe the MWE usage and concreteness. The correlations between those and the CEFR levels are shown in Table 2 (absolute values lower than 0.26 and those with p-value>0.05 are not shown in Table 2). We also highlight that some separation statistical measures, such as minimum (Min) and first quartile (Q1), are better descriptors than the average one for MWEs concreteness. Moreover, we identified that the correlation between the levels and the number of words corrected by the MWE occurrence is 0.82.

MWE	Kurt	Q3	Median	Q1	Min
CONC	0.40	-0.29	-0.35	-0.37	-0.50
CNT	-	-0.02	-	-	-

Table 2: Correlation of MWE features aggregators

[8]Average, sum, minimum, maximum, length and mode as measures of range and tendency. Median, variance, standard deviation, relative standard deviation, dolch, first and third quartile, eighth and ninth percentiles and interquartile range as measures of dispersion and separation. Skewness and kurtosis for description of the curve.

4.3. Classification

For exploring the relationship between the scores, we resort to feature-based machine learning. We explored the relation inter-families by combining the different scores that compose each of the 14 families (see Section 3) as features for predicting the CEFR level of an essay. Since some families are strongly related, we also explore the combination of them as features. In other words, we combined *parser* (MOR, POS, DEP, PRH and TNS), and lexical norms-based (NRM and MWE_{conc}) features (NRM_{all}). In addition, for the sake of comparison, we considered the occurrence of MWE and their concreteness as individual features. Finally, we combined all features (*all*) to identify the full prediction capacity of a model trained using all features described in this work. For comparing the impact of the MWE features in this set of all features, we removed the MWE features from the training. Aiming to avoid bias of a specific model, we explored two machine learning models, one based on classification (Random Forest; RF) and the other on regression (Simple Logistic; SL). All these models were trained using stratified cross-validation 10 folds. The average[9] and standard deviation results of these models using the different feature sets are shown in Table 4.

For the SL, the results by feature family indicate that the best results are obtained when using the DVR features, in line with the results of the correlation study (Section 4.2). However, the MOR features seem to be more informative when using the FR. This difference is probably related to the search strategy employed by the RF, which can better divide the search space.

The combination of different families had a remarkable positive effect on the parser-based features (increasing the F1 from 77% to 83% in the RF and the RMSE from 1.065 to 0.857 in the LR). The combination of lexical norms with the MWE concreteness showed a small improvement (p-value<0.05). Despite all these improvements by combining new features, the use of only DVR features achieved the best result in the regression. This again points to the need for an intricate search space strategy. Lastly, we did not observe a significant difference between the use of all features and all except the MWE-related features.

5. Conclusions

In this work, we study MWE features to predict essay scores. Concreteness of the MWEs found per level leads us to believe that MWE concreteness has an impact to predict essay scores. However, the correlation and machine learning results do not confirm it. MWE has been studied in other languages, such as French François and Watrin (2011) who observed similar results. In future work, the approach proposed by Wilkens et al. (2022) can be included in the feature's

[9]The standard deviation RMSE is below 0.02 and for the other scores below 0.01.

Family	best score	general				by nationality	
		rank		corr		rank	
		best	family	best	family	best	family
DVR	STTR (all surface tks)	1	138.9 (120.8)	0.81	0.42 (0.25)	2.0 (0.8)	137.9 (117.4)
DEV	depth	25	95.1 (77.5)	0.70	0.48 (0.17)	25.0 (0.0)	97.3 (78.7)
DEP	mark	26	194.5 (126.5)	0.62	0.29 (0.20)	29.7 (4.7)	198.7 (125.1)
POS	punct	35	204.3 (90.0)	0.59	0.27 (0.14)	35.1 (7.0)	214.6 (92.9)
LEN	word per sent.	36	66.8 (28.3)	0.58	0.50 (0.07)	39.5 (12.3)	66.9 (25.6)
NRM	AOA	42	105.6 (66.9)	0.58	0.43 (0.13)	41.2 (5.9)	107.7 (68.1)
FRQ	content words subtlex	44	198.0 (107.8)	0.57	0.28 (0.18)	42.1 (5.1)	199 (107.5)
PRH	SBAR	52	254.1 (103.8)	0.54	0.20 (0.16)	52.5 (6.9)	252.0 (100.8)
TNS	use past	63	266.0 (85.0)	0.51	0.18 (0.12)	64.1 (3.6)	267.7 (84.4)
MOR	finite verb	69	204.4 (94.4)	0.47	0.26 (0.14)	77.5 (14.8)	215.3 (97.1)
NGH	phonologic dist	71	254.3 (118.1)	0.47	0.20 (0.17)	71.5 (8.7)	247.8 (113.2)
SOP	verbs	75	163.8 (88.8)	0.46	0.32 (0.14)	78.7 (12.2)	166.6 (93.5)
MWE	MWE_{conc}	142	-	0.36	-	136.7 (18.9)	-
COH	PPMI (lemma)	183	291.5 (68.3)	0.29	0.14 (0.09)	188.9 (25.4)	288.7 (59.4)
GRD	C1	213	235.6 (28.5)	0.24	0.21 (0.04)	212.2 (14.4)	237.6 (28.8)
MWE	MWE_{cnt}	233	-	0.21	-	239.9 (18.4)	-

Table 3: Correlation of different features and families of features considering the entire corpus and the learners' nationalities

Feature set	RandForest		SLogistic	
	ACC	F1	MAE	RMSE
LEN	0.553	0.553	0.897	1.364
FRQ	0.682	0.682	0.739	1.200
GRD	0.490	0.490	1.014	1.487
NGH	0.561	0.560	1.053	1.520
NRM	0.624	0.624	0.744	1.158
SOP	0.498	0.498	0.869	1.294
DVR	0.745	0.745	0.410	0.789
DEP	0.736	0.736	0.630	1.065
PRH	0.645	0.645	0.941	1.406
DEV	0.726	0.726	0.694	1.075
POS	0.745	0.744	0.772	1.235
MOR	0.775	0.775	0.682	1.126
TNS	0.565	0.559	0.731	1.161
COH	0.519	0.519	1.170	1.628
MWE	0.428	0.425	1.455	1.916
MWE_{cnt}	0.454	0.447	1.660	2.121
MWE_{conc}	0.418	0.413	1.499	1.946
Parser	0.835	0.835	0.425	0.857
NRM_{all}	0.640	0.640	0.734	1.153
All	0.843	0.843	0.535	0.697
All-MWE	0.844	0.844	0.534	0.699

Table 4: Results of the machine learning models using different feature sets

creation since we observed different behavior per level that are identified by statistical descriptors other than average. Therefore, it might lead to a better understanding of the learner's usage of MWE and its applicability for essay scoring.

6. Acknowledgements

This research has been partially funded by a research convention with France Éducation International. Computational resources have been provided by the Consortium des Équipements de Calcul Intensif (CÉCI), funded by the Fonds de la Recherche Scientifique de Belgique (F.R.S.-FNRS) under Grant No. 2.5020.11 and by the Walloon Region.

7. Bibliographical References

Adamchik, V. A., Hyclak, T. J., Sedlak, P., and Taylor, L. W. (2019). Wage returns to english proficiency in poland. *Journal of Labor Research*, 40(3):276–295.

Alexopoulou, T., Michel, M., Murakami, A., and Meurers, D. (2017). Task effects on linguistic complexity and accuracy: A large-scale learner corpus analysis employing natural language processing techniques. *Language Learning*, 67(S1):180–208.

Arnaud, P. J. and Béjoint, H. (1992). *Vocabulary and applied linguistics*. Springer.

Arnold, T., Ballier, N., Gaillat, T., and Lissón, P. (2018). Predicting cefrl levels in learner english on the basis of metrics and full texts. *arXiv preprint arXiv:1806.11099*.

Arnon, I. and Snider, N. (2010). More than words: Frequency effects for multi-word phrases. *Journal of memory and language*, 62(1):67–82.

Balikas, G. (2018). Lexical bias in essay level prediction. *arXiv preprint arXiv:1809.08935*.

Ballier, N., Gaillat, T., Simpkin, A., Stearns, B., Bouyé, M., and Zarrouk, M. (2019). A supervised learning model for the automatic assessment of language levels based on learner errors. In *European Conference* on *Technology Enhanced Learning*, pages 308–320. Springer.

Ballier, N., Canu, S., Petitjean, C., Gasso, G., Balhana, C., Alexopoulou, T., and Gaillat, T. (2020). Machine learning for learner english: A plea for creating learner data challenges. *International Journal of Learner Corpus Research*, 6(1):72–103.

Berzak, Y., Kenney, J., Spadine, C., Wang, J. X., Lam, L., Mori, K. S., Garza, S., and Katz, B. (2016). Universal dependencies for learner english. *arXiv preprint arXiv:1605.04278*.

Boyd, M. and Cao, X. (2009). Immigrant language proficiency, earnings, and language policies. *Canadian Studies in Population [ARCHIVES]*, 36(1-2):63–86.

Bullinaria, J. A. and Levy, J. P. (2007). Extracting semantic representations from word co-occurrence statistics: A computational study. *Behavior research methods*, 39(3):510–526.

Calzolari, N., Fillmore, C. J., Grishman, R., Ide, N., Lenci, A., MacLeod, C., and Zampolli, A. (2002). Towards best practice for multiword expressions in computational lexicons. In *LREC*, volume 2, pages 1934–1940.

Carroll, J. B. (1964). Language and thought. *Reading Improvement*, 2(1):80.

Chaudron, C. and Parker, K. (1990). Discourse markedness and structural markedness: The acquisition of English noun phrases. *Studies in second language acquisition*, 12(1):43–64.

Chen, X. and Meurers, D. (2016). Ctap: A web-based tool supporting automatic complexity analysis. In *Proceedings of the workshop on computational linguistics for linguistic complexity (CL4LC)*, pages 113–119.

Chen, X., Alexopoulou, T., and Tsimpli, I. (2021). Automatic extraction of subordinate clauses and its application in second language acquisition research. *Behavior Research Methods*, 53(2):803–817.

Covington, M. A. and McFall, J. D. (2010). Cutting the gordian knot: The moving-average type–token ratio (mattr). *Journal of quantitative linguistics*, 17(2):94–100.

Dahlmann, I. and Adolphs, S. (2007). Pauses as an indicator of psycholinguistically valid multi-word expressions (mwes)? In *Proceedings of the workshop on a broader perspective on multiword expressions*, pages 49–56.

Dale, E. and Chall, J. S. (1948). A formula for predicting readability: Instructions. *Educational research bulletin*, pages 37–54.

Du, X., Afzaal, M., and Al Fadda, H. (2022). Collocation use in efl learners' writing across multiple language proficiencies: A corpus-driven study. *Frontiers in Psychology*, 13:752134–752134.

François, T. and Watrin, P. (2011). On the contribution of mwe-based features to a readability formula for french as a foreign language. In *Proceedings of the International Conference Recent Advances in Natural Language Processing 2011*, pages 441–447.

Gaillat, T., Simpkin, A., Ballier, N., Stearns, B., Sousa, A., Bouyé, M., and Zarrouk, M. (2021). Predicting cefr levels in learners of english: the use of microsystem criterial features in a machine learning approach. *ReCALL*, pages 1–17.

Garner, J. R. (2016). A phrase-frame approach to investigating phraseology in learner writing across proficiency levels. *International Journal of Learner Corpus Research*, 2(1):31–67.

Glucksberg, S. (1989). Metaphors in conversation: How are they understood? why are they used? *Metaphor and Symbol*, 4(3):125–143.

Graesser, A. C., McNamara, D. S., Louwerse, M. M., and Cai, Z. (2004). Coh-metrix: Analysis of text on cohesion and language. *Behavior research methods, instruments, & computers*, 36(2):193–202.

Guiraud, P. (1959). *Problèmes et méthodes de la statistique linguistique*, volume 2. D. Reidel.

Heafield, K., Pouzyrevsky, I., Clark, J. H., and Koehn, P. (2013). Scalable modified Kneser-Ney language model estimation. In *Proceedings of the 51st Annual Meeting of the Association for Computational Linguistics (Volume 2: Short Papers)*, pages 690–696.

Herdan, G. (1960). *Type-token mathematics*, volume 4. Mouton.

Herdan, G. (1966). *The advanced theory of language as choice and chance*. Springer Berlin.

Jackendoff, R. (1997). Twistin'the night away. *Language*, pages 534–559.

Jung, Y., Crossley, S., and McNamara, D. (2019). Predicting second language writing proficiency in learner texts using computational tools. *The Journal of Asia TEFL*, 16(1):37–52.

Kitaev, N., Cao, S., and Klein, D. (2019). Multilingual constituency parsing with self-attention and pre-training. In *Proceedings of the 57th Annual Meeting of the Association for Computational Linguistics*, pages 3499–3505, Florence, Italy, July. Association for Computational Linguistics.

Kneser, R. and Ney, H. (1995). Improved backing-off for m-gram language modeling. In *1995 international conference on acoustics, speech, and signal processing*, volume 1, pages 181–184. IEEE.

Kyle, K. (2016). *Measuring syntactic development in L2 writing: Fine grained indices of syntactic complexity and usage-based indices of syntactic sophistication*. Ph.D. thesis, Georgia State University, Atlanta, Georgia.

Lan, G., Zhang, Q., Lucas, K., Sun, Y., and Gao, J. (2022). A corpus-based investigation on noun phrase complexity in l1 and l2 english writing. *English for Specific Purposes*, 67:4–17.

Lu, X. (2010). Automatic analysis of syntactic complexity in second language writing. *International journal of corpus linguistics*, 15(4):474–496.

Michel, M., Murakami, A., Alexopoulou, T., and

Meurers, D. (2019). Effects of task type on morphosyntactic complexity across proficiency: Evidence from a large learner corpus of a1 to c2 writings. *Instructed Second Language Acquisition*, 3(2):124–152.

Pendakur, K. and Pendakur, R. (2007). Colour my world: Have earnings gaps for canadianborn ethnic minorities changed over time?

Römer, U. and Berger, C. M. (2019). Observing the emergence of constructional knowledge: Verb patterns in german and spanish learners of english at different proficiency levels. *Studies in Second Language Acquisition*, 41(5):1089–1110.

Römer, U. (2019). A corpus perspective on the development of verb constructions in second language learners. *International Journal of Corpus Linguistics*, 24(3):268–290.

Sag, I. A., Baldwin, T., Bond, F., Copestake, A., and Flickinger, D. (2002). Multiword expressions: A pain in the neck for nlp. In *International conference on intelligent text processing and computational linguistics*, pages 1–15. Springer.

Srichanyachon, N. (2012). Teacher written feedback for l2 learners' writing development. *Humanities, Arts and Social Sciences Studies (Former Name Silpakorn University Journal of Social Sciences, Humanities, and Arts)*, pages 7–17.

Stolcke, A. (2002). Srilm-an extensible language modeling toolkit. In *Seventh international conference on spoken language processing*.

Stubbs, M. (2007). An example of frequent english phraseology: distributions, structures and functions. In *Corpus linguistics 25 years on*, pages 87–105. Brill.

Tack, A., François, T., Roekhaut, S., and Fairon, C. (2017). Human and automated cefr-based grading of short answers. In *Proceedings of the 12th Workshop on Innovative Use of NLP for Building Educational Applications*, pages 169–179.

Tono, Y. (2013). Automatic extraction of l2 criterial lexico-grammatical features across pseudo-longitudinal learner corpora: using edit distance and variability-based neighbour clustering. *L2 vocabulary acquisition, knowledge and use*, pages 149–176.

Vajjala, S. (2018). Automated assessment of non-native learner essays: Investigating the role of linguistic features. *International Journal of Artificial Intelligence in Education*, 28(1):79–105.

Weigle, S. C. (2013). English language learners and automated scoring of essays: Critical considerations. *Assessing Writing*, 18(1):85–99.

Wilkens, R., Alfter, D., Wang, X., Pintard, A., Tack, A., Yancey, K., and François, T. (2022). Fabra: French aggregator-based readability assessment toolkit. In *Language Resources and Evaluation Conference (LREC)*.

Wray, A. (1999). Formulaic language in learners and native speakers. *Language teaching*, 32(4):213–231.

Wray, A. (2002). *Formulaic language and the lexicon*. ERIC.

Yannakoudakis, H., Briscoe, T., and Medlock, B. (2011). A new dataset and method for automatically grading esol texts. In *Proceedings of the 49th annual meeting of the association for computational linguistics: human language technologies*, pages 180–189.

Yngve, V. H. (1960). A model and an hypothesis for language structure. *Proceedings of the American philosophical society*, 104(5):444–466.

Zilio, L., Wilkens, R., and Fairon, C. (2018). Investigating productive and receptive knowledge: A profile for second language learning. In *Proceedings of the 27th International Conference on Computational Linguistics*, pages 3467–3478.

8. Language Resource References

Baroni, M., Bernardini, S., Ferraresi, A., and Zanchetta, E. (2009). The WaCky wide web: A collection of very large linguistically processed web-crawled corpora. *Language resources and evaluation*, 43(3):209–226.

Bartlett, S., Kondrak, G., and Cherry, C. (2009). On the syllabification of phonemes. In *Proceedings of human language technologies: The 2009 annual conference of the north american chapter of the association for computational linguistics*, pages 308–316.

Brysbaert, M. and New, B. (2009). Moving beyond kučera and francis: A critical evaluation of current word frequency norms and the introduction of a new and improved word frequency measure for american english. *Behavior research methods*, 41(4):977–990.

Coltheart, M. (1981). The mrc psycholinguistic database. *The Quarterly Journal of Experimental Psychology Section A*, 33(4):497–505.

Dürlich, L. and François, T. (2018). Efllex: A graded lexical resource for learners of english as a foreign language. In *Proceedings of the Eleventh International Conference on Language Resources and Evaluation (LREC 2018)*.

Geertzen, J., Alexopoulou, T., and Korhonen, A. (2013). Automatic linguistic annotation of large scale l2 databases: The ef-cambridge open language database (efcamdat). *Selected Proceedings of the 31st Second Language Research Forum (SLRF), Cascadilla Press, MA*.

Muraki, E., Abdalla, S., Brysbaert, M., and Pexman, P. (2022). Concreteness ratings for 62 thousand english multiword expressions. 03.

Qi, P., Zhang, Y., Zhang, Y., Bolton, J., and Manning, C. D. (2020). Stanza: A python natural language processing toolkit for many human languages. *arXiv preprint arXiv:2003.07082*.

Author Index

Association for Computational Linguistics
209 N. Eighth Street
Stroudsburg, Pennsylvania 18360

ISBN 978-1-7138-6144-7

9 781713 861447

CURRAN ASSOCIATES INC.
proceedings.com

1st Workshop on Formalisms and Methodology for Learning by Reading 2010

(FAM-LbR)

Held at NAACL HLT 2010

Los Angeles, California, USA
6 June 2010

ISBN: 978-1-61738-678-7